Proprietary Schools:
Programs, Policies, and Prospects

by John B. Lee and Jamie P. Merisotis

ASHE-ERIC Higher Education Report 5, 199

Prepared by

*Clearinghouse on Higher Education
The George Washington University*

In cooperation with

*Association for the Study
of Higher Education*

Published by

*School of Education and Human Development
The George Washington University*

Jonathan D. Fife, Series Editor

Cite as

Lee, John B., and Jamie P. Merisotis. 1990. *Proprietary Schools: Programs, Policies, and Prospects.* ASHE-ERIC Higher Education Report No. 5. Washington, D.C.: The George Washington University, School of Education and Human Development.

Library of Congress Catalog Card Number 91-60263
ISSN 0884-0040
ISBN 1-878380-02-8

Managing Editor: Bryan Hollister
Manuscript Editor: Barbara Fishel/Editech
Cover design by Michael David Brown, Rockville, Maryland

$L C 1045$
$.L 514$
1990

The ERIC Clearinghouse on Higher Education invites individuals to submit proposals for writing monographs for the *ASHE-ERIC Higher Education Report* series. Proposals must include:
1. A detailed manuscript proposal of not more than five pages.
2. A chapter-by-chapter outline.
3. A 75-word summary to be used by several review committees for the initial screening and rating of each proposal.
4. A vita and a writing sample.

ERIC Clearinghouse on Higher Education
School of Education and Human Development
The George Washington University
One Dupont Circle, Suite 630
Washington, DC 20036-1183

This publication was prepared partially with funding from the Office of Educational Research and Improvement, U.S. Department of Education, under contract no. ED RI-88-062014. The opinions expressed in this report do not necessarily reflect the positions or policies of OERI or the Department.

EXECUTIVE SUMMARY

Proprietary schools or, as they are sometimes called, "private career schools," are not well known or understood for several reasons. First, they have developed outside the traditional education community and are often owned and operated by business people who are more comfortable in the world of commerce than the education community. Second, no data are commonly collected and reported on schools in the sector. As a result, only scattered and inconsistent reports are available on even the simplest census information. Third, academic researchers in the education field have largely ignored the sector.

How Have Private Career Schools Evolved?

Colleges in the colonial era did not teach the practical arts, such as navigation and accounting; those skills were taught by private masters, often in their homes. Business skills, including penmanship, shorthand, and bookkeeping, made up the bulk of early private career school curricula. It was not until after World War II, when the needs of increasing technology and a complex workplace began to outstrip the traditional apprenticeship program's ability to supply the needs of industry, that proprietary schools began to expand in the trade and technical fields.

Since World War II, the growth of private career schools has been closely related to changes in federal student aid policy. Starting with the Veterans Education Benefits program after World War II and continuing to today's student aid program, proprietary school students have used government student grants and loans. The watershed 1972 Amendments to the Higher Education Act provided full and equal participation with traditional higher education students. Along with that use have come concerns about the quality of the programs offered, the way they are advertised, and the ethics of school owners. Charges and countercharges about the appropriateness of private career schools' participation in federal student aid programs lie at the heart of today's increasing interest in the sector.

What Is the Role of Proprietary Schools and Traditional Higher Education?

Private career schools differ from traditional higher education in several important ways. Many offer programs lasting less than a year and do not grant degrees, although nearly 300 private career schools, a sizable exception, offer at least an

---

AA degree. The greatest similarity, in terms of students' characteristics and curricula, is with community colleges, which often offer vocational education programs similar to private career schools.

The differences between private career schools and traditional colleges and universities are more easily identified. At the core of the difference is the goal of realizing a profit for private owners. Proprietary schools have placed decision making in the hands of the owner, with no tradition of faculty senate or collegial decision making. Teaching positions are less permanent, because instructors have no tenure. Private career schools tend to be more sensitive to market forces than traditional colleges and, because they lack a time-consuming and limiting system of governance, can shift quickly to meet the needs of employers and the interests of students. Proprietary schools are less likely to have a board of trustees.

This double-edged argument cuts both ways. Critics cite private career schools' profit motive and lack of procedures for institutional accountability as potential causes of under-investing in the educational program and enrolling students merely to take advantage of public student aid programs. Supporters argue that proprietary schools have become a cost-effective way to deliver education to a community of students that traditional colleges have not served well, maintaining that private career schools provide diversity and energetic competition for traditional colleges.

What Curricula Do Private Career Schools Offer?
Private career schools offer literally hundreds of programs. The majority of students enroll in office, technology, and personal service programs. The technical areas are dominated by auto mechanics and computer-related fields, but courses of study run the gamut from broadcast technology to architectural engineering.

The curricula in private career schools are more structured and oriented toward job skills than usually found in traditional colleges. All students in a program generally take the same sequence of courses, with a new class starting as quickly as every two or three weeks. Much more hands-on education is available, with less emphasis on theory than in the collegiate sector. Programs whose students are eligible for federal student aid range from 300 hours to graduate degrees.

How Many Students Are Enrolled in Private Career Schools and What Are Their Characteristics?

Enrollments in private career schools vary from four to over 6,000 students in any one school; the average enrollment is just under 400, the modal enrollment just over 100. Thus, the typical private career school is considerably smaller than a traditional college, with staff numbering as few as five or six people. In total, the 4,000 accredited schools enroll an estimated 1.8 million students, up from 1.4 million in 1987. In addition, 1.5 million students in home study schools are not included in most of the statistics describing the sector. (These numbers do not include enrollments in nonaccredited schools.)

Proprietary schools are located close to their students, which means they are generally in highly populated areas. Most students live at home while attending school, for private career schools often do not provide residential facilities for students.

Despite the diversity of students and programs in private career schools, they share some general characteristics. Private career school students differ from average students in other postsecondary sectors in several ways:

- In general, they are older and more likely to be independent of their parents' income.
- Their academic skills and high school preparation are weaker.
- They are from lower socioeconomic backgrounds.
- They are more likely to be female and minority.

On average, they are most similar to students in community colleges.

Business, cosmetology, and technology programs dominate the enrollment in private career schools, most of which attract a large number of females. The trade and technical fields enroll fewer students, but the majority are male.

What Are the Outcomes of Private Career School Education?

Completion rates and estimates of the number who fail to finish a program of study vary depending on the measures used. The best estimate is that just over 60 percent of the students enrolling in private career schools receive a certificate or degree, compared to just over 40 percent for students in community colleges (although some community college students never intend to receive a certificate or a degree).

In the short run, earnings of proprietary school graduates are similar to graduates from community college vocational programs, but little information is available about the longer-term effects on income of attending a private career school.

Private career school students report a high degree of satisfaction with their education, but a higher proportion of previously enrolled students report dissatisfaction with their education, compared with traditional college students. They are also more likely to report periods of unemployment than students attending other types of schools.

What Policy Issues Affect Private Career School Education?

In the mid-1980s, proprietary school students were identified as having higher default rates on student loans than borrowers from other sectors, and researchers found that over a quarter of federal student aid was going to students in private career schools. These findings triggered old concerns about consumer abuses in the sector and charges that proprietary school graduates were not well qualified for employment. Critics contend that high defaults in the sector are a result of poor programs, citing the high correlation of sudden school closings and default rates.

On the other hand, private career schools enroll students with higher potential risk for default compared to traditional college students. Some analysts attribute the higher rates of default to the inherent risk of students who face higher odds of succeeding and have less experience with the subtleties of repaying a loan.

Charges that proprietary schools violate basic principles of fair advertising and mislead potential students are supported by anecdotal evidence, but no research suggests that these practices are prevalent throughout the sector.

The increasing concern about the quality of education offered by private career schools has led to considering the reform of state licensing and private accreditation requirements, but the appropriate role of these two entities in ensuring program quality is not well understood. State licensing and oversight vary widely among the states, from perfunctory to very specific. Licensing has three purposes: (1) to ensure applicants that a school meets minimum education standards, (2) to protect the state's financial interests in the school, and (3) to constrain unfair business practices.

One major interest of the states is ensuring students a tuition refund or continuation of their education if a school closes suddenly or declares bankruptcy. Most state oversight of proprietary schools, however, suffers from lack of enforcement and review staff.

Private accreditation was originally a voluntary activity designed to help institutions achieve and maintain educational quality; more recently, however, it has performed as a "gatekeeper." To participate in federal student aid programs, a school must be accredited by an organization recognized by the Department of Education. This dual responsibility has put new pressures on accreditation, to help improve education and to extend regulatory constraints on the operation of a school.

What Are the Implications?
As a newly visible and little understood participant in postsecondary education, private career schools pose a challenge to traditional colleges and universities in the continuing competition among schools for public funds and students. If the questions about quality and ethics can be answered, these schools can provide education to a new community of students not often served by existing colleges and universities without the doubts and criticism marking the sector today.

ADVISORY BOARD

Alberto Calbrera
Arizona State University

Carol Everly Floyd
Board of Regents of the Regency Universities System
State of Illinois

Judy Gappa
San Francisco State University

George Keller
University of Pennsylvania

J. Fredericks Volkwein
State University of New York

Bobby Wright
Pennsylvania State University

Ami Zusman
University of California

CONSULTING EDITORS

Brenda M. Albright
State of Tennessee Higher Education Commission

Walter R. Allen
University of California

Leonard L. Baird
University of Kentucky

James H. Banning
Colorado State University

Trudy W. Banta
University of Tennessee

Margaret J. Barr
Texas Christian University

Rita Bornstein
University of Miami

Larry Braskamp
University of Illinois

Paul T. Brinkman
National Center for Higher Education Management Systems

Robert F. Carbone
University of Maryland

Jay L. Chronister
University of Virginia

Mary E. Dilworth
ERIC Clearinghouse on Teacher Education

James A. Eison
Southeast Missouri State University

Valerie French
American University

Edward R. Hines
Illinois State University

Joseph V. Julian
Syracuse University

Jeanne M. Likens
Ohio State University

REVIEW PANEL

Charles Adams
University of Amherst

Richard Alfred
University of Michigan

Philip G. Altbach
State University of New York

Louis C. Attinasi, Jr.
University of Houston

Ann E. Austin
Vanderbilt University

Robert J. Barak
State Board of Regents

Alan Bayer
Virginia Polytechnic Institute and State University

John P. Bean
Indiana University

Louis W. Bender
Florida State University

Carol Bland
University of Minnesota

Deane G. Bornheimer
New York University

John A. Centra
Syracuse University

Arthur W. Chickering
George Mason University

Jay L. Chronister
University of Virginia

Mary Jo Clark
San Juan Community College

Shirley M. Clark
University of Minnesota

Darrel A. Clowes
Virginia Polytechnic Institute and State University

Robert G. Cope
University of Washington

John W. Creswell
University of Nebraska

Richard Duran
University of California

Larry H. Ebbers
Iowa State University

Kenneth C. Green
University of Southern California

Edward R. Hines
Illinois State University

George D. Kuh
Indiana University

James R. Mingle
State Higher Education Executive Officers

Michael T. Nettles
University of Tennessee

Pedro Reyes
University of Wisconsin

H. Bradley Sagen
University of Iowa

CONTENTS

FOREWORD

If it is to more fully understand the changing educational demands of our society, higher education must have an accurate understanding of the proprietary sector of postsecondary education. By ignoring the existence of proprietary institutions or attempting to segregate their activities from the mainstream, nonprofit institutions miss an opportunity to further awareness of their changing mission.

Proprietary institutions, or private career schools as they are also called, have come under increased criticism for a number of reasons. As more data become available on the high number of students entering private career schools and qualifying for the various student financial aid programs, nonprofit institutions exhibit a heightened anxiety over the competition for the decreasing number of college-going students. Because the educational mission and control over curricula are considerably different for proprietary schools, the collegiate sector is highly suspicious about their educational legitimacy. The suspicion is further increased when comparing the lengths of programs at private career schools—two months to two years—with those of traditional higher education—two to eight years. All this anxiety and suspicion is often based on surface impressions and general misunderstanding.

This report by John B. Lee, president of JBL Associates, and Jamie P. Merisotis, public policy consultant, offers the most comprehensive examination available on the proprietary school sector. It describes the history and present state of proprietary schools, their pros and cons as well as basic information about the schools, programs, and students, and offers recommendations for further study.

Proprietary education has long been part of our education system. To deny or belittle its existence does very little to ensure that all sectors of postsecondary education serve society well. Private career schools not only complement and supplement collegiate higher education but also, because of their ability to be more responsive, often serve as early indicators of changing educational demands. This report contributes significantly to an increasing understanding of their role.

Jonathan D. Fife
Professor and Director
ERIC Clearinghouse on Higher Education

PREFACE

This is a volume whose publication is probably long overdue. We do not mean to suggest that no other authors could have accomplished what we do within these pages or even that we have had the idea to publish such a book for quite some time. Instead, we refer only to the need for a review of the literature on proprietary schools, given their importance in postsecondary education policy, especially at the federal level. The debate about proprietary schools that was rekindled in the mid-1980s and continues to the present would have been much more informed and informative had this work existed.

We believe that much is at stake in the current discussions about the future of proprietary school education and specifically the support that the federal government should provide. Future decisions could affect some 2 million current students and involve billions of dollars. In this environment, it is important that policy makers and those who influence them be fully informed about the strengths and weaknesses of proprietary schools and how they compare to other types of education, based on existing research.

This interest in informing those who have concerns about proprietary school education but who do not fully understand its dimensions has brought us together on this monograph. Even though we each have independent views about the future role that proprietary schools should play in post-secondary education—views frequently contradictory with the other's opinion—we have attempted, to the best of our abilities, to put such value judgments aside. The urgent need for informed decision making demands that we put aside our differences.

While we might disagree about the meaning of certain data or the correctness of various views, we are in complete agreement on one central point: Few in the public policy arena truly understand the nature of proprietary school training or the role that it plays in postsecondary education. This book has therefore been written to help those who influence and make policy understand what proprietary schools are and what they do.

This volume explores such fundamental issues as the historical context for proprietary school education, similarities and differences between proprietary schools and traditional higher education, demographic and other characteristics about the schools and their students, curricula, and staffing. It also discusses existing data and research on probably the most explosive issue in policy debates: measures of performance and outcomes, or what can broadly be described as the "quality" of proprietary school education.

For those who are interested in micro-policy, we also briefly examine the questions that have been most repeatedly asked in recent years: What role does student aid play for proprietary school students? How do accreditation and state licensing fit into the overall regulation of proprietary school education? The monograph concludes with a summary and discussion of the relationship among the various players with a direct interest in proprietary school education—students, the federal government, state governments, and accrediting agencies.

As the reader will find, much remains to be learned about proprietary schools, their place in postsecondary education, and their contributions to the labor market. We share the frustration of those who feel this literature review lacks depth of analysis on many critical issues. If the publication of this monograph compels concerned and interested researchers to take up this topic in a meaningful way, we will have accomplished much of what we had hoped to do.

John B. Lee   **Jamie P. Merisotis**

ACKNOWLEDGMENTS

We extend our thanks to Bill Carson and Henry Herzing, who reviewed early versions of the report, and Wellford Wilms, Richard Moore, Christopher Davis, and James Mingle for their helpful comments on the complete manuscript. The comments of all reviewers were both useful and instructive.

We would also like to thank the Career Training Foundation of Washington, D.C., which funded some of the research and writing of this monograph. Jon Fife and the staff of ASHE-ERIC associated with the ongoing production of this report series have also been generous with their patience and cooperation.

Special thanks go to Linda Shafer, who spent endless hours tracking down errant documents, checking the sources, and carefully editing the manuscript. Her help was invaluable in completing this project.

INTRODUCTION

Since the middle 1980s, increased attention has been focused on for-profit postsecondary occupational and trade schools, frequently referred to as "private career schools" or "proprietary institutions." (These terms are used interchangeably in this report.) This attention has resulted from a confluence of events, the most important being a rapid increase in the total dollar amount of federally guaranteed student loans entering default. The debate about default has resulted in a backlash against these schools, including tighter restrictions on some loans, a renewed focus on state licensing and accreditation, and suggestions of even more stringent restrictions, including development of a separate federal student aid program for vocational students.[1]

Such is the way of private career school education in this country. Proprietary schools have traditionally been, and continue to be, seen as outsiders in the world of postsecondary education. For many reasons, those in traditional higher education, government, and the media have approached these profit-making institutions with a combination of suspicion, mistrust, and outright disdain.

Consumers of proprietary school education—the students— have apparently seen the private career school sector through somewhat different lenses. In the last century, these schools have developed and flourished despite sporadic cycles of critical journalistic reports and reviews highlighting consumer abuse, fraud, and low graduation rates. Today, more students than ever are enrolling in private career schools in an expanding number of fields.

Why are the views so disparate? This monograph explores this question by examining the existing literature on proprietary schools—literature that, while scant in several critical areas, needs to be reviewed and understood by those who make and influence governmental policy. It is not the purpose of this monograph to determine who is "right" in the debate

[Various groups] have approached these profit-making institutions with a combination of suspicion, mistrust, and outright disdain.

---

1. This review is limited to those schools that are eligible to participate in federal student aid programs, which include only institutions that are accredited and offer programs of at least 300 hours. Literally thousands of proprietary schools do not fit into this category, for example, avocational programs, such as ballroom dancing or a pilot's license (training for a commercial pilot's license is eligible); short programs, such as learning to use computer software programs and studying for the state real estate or insurance exams; and schools that participate only in job training programs and do not receive federal student aid.

about the proper position private career schools should assume in postsecondary education. Instead, its aim is to arm the combatants with the necessary weapons to debate the issues from a well-informed position. The exaggerated claims made on both sides of this question, it is hoped, will be reduced by the evidence presented in this monograph.

Most of what is currently being debated in the policy arena is not really new in any real sense. For many of the contentious issues, today's discussion is simply a second or third round, perhaps best illustrated by two competing views of private career school education voiced more than half a century ago. The first, in a 1930 book by Herman S. Hall, a prominent vocational educator and proprietary school critic, argues the case against private career schools in a tone whose echoes can still be heard today:

> *Some such schools are providing real training, but unfortunately many make extravagant claims . . . they cannot fulfill. . . . It is a reprehensible act to prey upon serious young men and women who wish to make something of themselves, and take their naturally limited capital under the misrepresentation that in return they are to receive training qualifying them for highly paid positions* (Hall 1930, pp. 40–41).

The second view, written by Herbert A. Tonne, a contemporary of Hall's, stands in stark contrast.

> *The United States recognizes and approves of the profit motive. If a private school can render a service equal to, and in some cases superior to, the public schools, and if students find sufficient justification for enrolling in it, then it is a worthy element in the American system of education* (Tonne 1939, p. 265).

Given the clear battle lines drawn between supporters and critics of proprietary schools today, both Hall and Tonne were less than successful at making their conceptions about proprietary schools become the standards by which all would be judged.

Today's battles have historical precedent, and they cover several issues: the apparent level of government support of private career school training, the ability of students to benefit from attending proprietary schools, and the outcomes of the education. Lessons learned from these historical examples could help pave the way toward an equitable and practical solution to the dilemmas currently plaguing American postsecondary education in general and proprietary school education in particular.

It is important to stress at the outset, however, that this report is not about the history of proprietary school education or the people and events that influenced its growth—though it does take account of both of these themes. Rather, it is about the current world in which private career schools exist and the lessons to be learned from research and analysis about the issues. History provides the framework with which contemporary research can be reviewed and evaluated. Current research provides evidence with which to examine conceptions and inform decision making.

Indeed, this monograph is very much about the present. It discusses those studies or pieces of data in the literature that reveal something important, useful, or interesting about proprietary schools. It seeks to inform those who have some interest in postsecondary education policies, but, the authors hope, it also is of interest to those with no immediate concerns about the implications of the research for public policy purposes.

This section is a primer on the private career school sector in general. It examines differences and similarities between private career schools and traditional institutions of higher education and discusses fundamentals regarding the curricula at these schools, the size and location of institutions, staffing and pay, and basic characteristics of the students who attend. First, however, it explores the historical context for today's proprietary schools.

Historical Context

The contemporary controversy over the role private vocational schools should play in postsecondary education is rooted in the history of their development and the cyclical concerns that are raised about whether for-profit enterprises should provide education and training. While much of the furor over private career school education may seem like a recent phenomenon, it is, in fact, part of a decades-long tradition of divergent opinions about these schools. This subsection concerns itself with the historical traditions that have made these schools what they are today. It reviews those events and facts that have helped to contribute to proprietary school education in its current manifestation.

The early history of proprietary school education

Much like their modern successors, less is known about the earliest private career schools in the United States than one would hope. This situation is not only because keeping records was less common in the period before World War II, but also because the "profit-making" status of some known schools has been difficult to determine. This discussion is confined to those schools cited in the literature that were known to have been private, for-profit institutions. And because so little information is known about trade and technical private career schools (as compared to private business schools), much of the information here necessarily refers only to those business schools.

Most authors in the literature on vocational education generally credit correspondence instruction as the first type of training to be conducted privately. A man named Caleb Philipps is known to have advertised a home study course in shorthand in the March 20, 1728, issue of *The Boston Gazette:*

> *Any Persons in the Country desirous to learn this Art, may by having the several Lessons sent Weekly to them, be as perfectly instructed as those that live in Boston* (Katz 1973, p. 6).

Private resident schools also became common sometime in the early and middle 18th century. These schools were operated by "proprietary masters," who conducted classes at a place of business or even in their homes. Like those who offered correspondence instruction, these proprietary masters advertised their services in newspapers and other periodicals. Courses of instruction included business programs, surveying, practical mathematics, and navigation (Katz 1973, p. 5).

The true growth of private vocational education that began in the early 19th century was anticipated by a growing need for persons skilled in trades and business. Mechanics' institutes began to spring up in several states. With the Lyceum Movement, patterned after the French system of popular education, came private schools dedicated entirely to practical instruction. Perhaps the earliest of these schools was the Gardner Lyceum in Maine, which opened in 1823. The school offered courses in farming, navigation, carpentry, and other subjects (ITT 1982, p. 44).

The earliest date for the beginning of the private business school is not known. Forbes Commercial School was the first school established to train students for a career in commerce (Petrello 1988). Others give credit to R.M. Bartlett, who established a school for bookkeeping instruction in Philadelphia in the 1820s and later expanded to Pittsburgh and Cincinnati (Herrick 1904; Hill 1920).[2] Other prominent names in the private business education field at the time included James Bennett of New York, Peter Duff of Pittsburgh, and Jonathan Jones of St. Louis. Many of these business school entrepreneurs offered instruction in accounting, bookkeeping, and penmanship. The rise of these schools can be traced to the rapid industrialization of the United States combined with the relative inefficiency of the apprentice system of training for business occupations (Tonne 1954, p. 403). Proprietary schools grew quickly between the early 1800s and the Civil War, and 15 to 20 private career schools had been established by the mid-1850s (Petrello 1988).

While early private career school owners responded to the marketplace by offering instruction in specific subjects to clients in one or more cities, none had the grand vision of their eventual successors. One who saw the big picture was R.C. Bacon, who founded Bacon's Mercantile Colleges sometime around 1850. Bacon's schools, with corporate organization and formal management structures, were located in Madison, Cleveland, and Cincinnati. Unfortunately, financial difficulties soon caused the collapse of the chain (Tonne 1954, p. 405).

The largest chain of proprietary schools during the middle 19th century was the Bryant-Stratton chain, founded by H.B. Bryant and H.D. Stratton. From its organization in 1852 through the end of the Civil War, the chain grew to over 50 schools in almost as many cities. The abbreviated story of the Bryant-Stratton chain is worth telling because of its parallels to the good and bad of today's private career school sector.

The chain was legally classified as a connected partnership arrangement, which allowed for reciprocity among schools.

---

2. Macmillan Publishers in New York produced several other books early in the 20th century that provide an excellent introduction to the roots of vocational and commercial education.

Instruction was based on a uniform system of lessons and text-books. "Scholarships"—actually just tuition payments—were sold to students and were usable at any of the schools.

Part of the problem with the chain arose through the use of the scholarships. Students quickly learned they could enroll in one school in a small town for a relatively low fee and then transfer to a school in a bigger city where the prospects for job placement were better. Unfortunately, this practice led to a situation where a significant percentage of the chain's total income went to the schools in the small towns, while the responsibility for training was left to the schools in the larger cities. Conflict among the local managers eventually culminated in the dissolution of the general partnership in 1867, the same year in which H.D. Stratton died. Some of the successors to the Bryant-Stratton schools still exist today, though in name only.

As several commentators have noted, the Bryant-Stratton chain was in many ways a model organization. Originally, the schools offered high-quality education in bookkeeping, pen-manship, and other subjects to a large number of students in many cities. The schools helped to fill an important need of the labor market not met by apprentice programs, high schools, or traditional colleges. Bryant-Stratton schools accepted students without regard to prior ability or aptitude.

Sadly, overexpansion turned a good business venture by two enterprising educators into an attempt to monopolize the industry. Stratton and Bryant dreamed of putting one of their schools in every city with a population over 10,000. This overzealous expansion gradually consumed the organization, however. Ability to pay became the only criterion for admission. Large sums of money were spent on advertising, including the use of gimmicks, such as brass bands and stump speeches upon the opening of a school. The organization thereby sought growth at an unrealistic pace and, combined with the dissatisfaction of the school managers in large cities because of the inequity in scholarships, eventually alienated proprietors and collapsed (Miller 1939, chap. 5).

Another mid-19th century educational entrepreneur and forerunner of today's proprietary school owner was H.G. Eastman, nephew of George W. Eastman, the photography pioneer. Learning from his uncle, H.G. Eastman became a master of marketing and spread schools across the nation. Many of his marketing methods are still in use today. For example, he effectively used advertising in newspapers and magazines to attract students, and, through the use of these and other methods, Eastman became a strong competitor with the Bryant-Stratton schools.

In the mid-1870s, an additional event helped propel private career schools to further success. The first key shift typewriter was displayed at the 1876 Centennial Exposition in Philadelphia. The machine was a sensation with businesses and soon resulted in sales of some 60,000 typewriters per year by the early 1890s, producing a huge demand for typists to operate the new machines. Proprietary schools developed to train the ever-growing ranks of future typists. Likewise, the need for persons skilled in shorthand also grew in importance, with Briton John Gregg bringing the system he invented to the United States (still the most widely used shorthand system today) (Bolino 1973, pp. 152–55).

During this post–Civil War period, traditional education was becoming more involved in practical education. In 1862, the Land Grant Act defined new applied arts and sciences as a mission for colleges and universities. The first public commercial high school was chartered in Washington, D.C., in 1890.

One of the most important, but often unrecognized, contributions of private business schools in the late 19th and early 20th centuries was their assistance in the career growth of women. Before the invention of the typewriter, most women who wanted to work were forced into a single occupation— teaching. During the Civil War, businesses were forced to use women as clerks for the first time. Business schools, however, recognized that women were an untapped source of students and therefore offered incentives for them to enroll. As early as 1890, the percentage of women students enrolled in proprietary and stenography schools exceeded that of men (Bolino 1973, pp. 152–55). Thus, in their own way, private business schools assisted the gradual progression of women's increased participation in the work force in the 20th century.

Statistics on who attended proprietary schools before World War II, or even how many students attended such schools, are virtually nonexistent. Much like collecting information from some proprietary schools today, the problem was not estimating how many schools or students existed at any one time but gaining responses to surveys. The percentage of schools reporting on U.S. Office of Education surveys of private business and commercial schools averaged less than 50 percent from 1876 to 1935 (when the Office ceased surveying the schools) (Bolino 1973). Thus, data from this period are likely to significantly underestimate the number of students enrolled.

From 1870 (the first year of the Office of Education's annual reports) to 1916 (the peak year of pre–World War I enroll-ments), the number of students in private business schools grew from 5,824 to 192,388. In that time, the number of schools in the survey grew from 26 to 912. Enrollments accel-erated in the postwar era to a peak of 336,032 in 1920, reflect-ing the return of ex-servicemen to civilian life. By the middle 1920s, however, enrollments had returned to their prewar lev-els (Bolino 1973, p. 163), largely because of the steady growth in high school vocational courses spurred by the passage of the Smith-Hughes Act in 1917.

The characteristics of students in proprietary schools also gradually began to change over time. One of the most impor-tant changes to occur in the first quarter of the century was the extent of academic preparation. Most of the students in the first dozen years of the century were high school drop-outs. By the early 1930s, however, 64 percent had graduated from high school. Likewise, while the number of men in pri-vate business schools exceeded the number of women until around 1915, by the late 1930s twice as many women as men were enrolled (Bolino 1973, p. 162). And women began to seek training in cosmetology. The popularity of "bobbed" hair required permanent waving that was beyond the ability of most women on their own (Lee and Munn 1988).

Proprietary school associations

One of the signals that private career schools were becoming increasingly important was the formation of national asso-ciations. This process started before World War I and con-tinued through the 1970s.

AICS. The Association of Independent Colleges and Schools is the oldest of the principal proprietary school associations. It began in 1912 with the founding of the National Association of Accredited Commercial Schools. The 23 founding members represented only a portion of the 155,000 students in private career schools at the time. In 1916, the association began meeting with federal government education policy makers to emphasize the role of private schools and to acquaint them with their concerns. These relations became particularly important during wartime expansions and postwar education for returning GIs.

In 1949, the National Association of Accredited Commercial Schools merged with the National Council of Business Schools to become the National Association and Council of Business Schools (NACBS). In 1962, the NACBS merged with the American Association of Commercial Colleges to become the United Business Schools Association (UBSA), with an institutional membership of 500 schools. The increasing importance of having representatives before Congress prompted the move in 1969 of its headquarters to Washington, D.C., where it continues to be located. In 1972, its name was changed to the Association of Independent Colleges and Schools.

NACCAS. The cosmetology schools association was founded in 1924 as an advocate for cosmetology schools before Congress and federal agencies. Today, the National Accrediting Commission of Cosmetology Arts and Sciences (NACCAS) is comprised of individual institutions, teachers, and associate members involved in cosmetology instruction. The association was formally chartered in 1985. Its current membership includes approximately 2,400 accredited and nonaccredited schools.

NATTS. The National Association of Trade and Technical Schools is a relative newcomer to the private career school associations. Formed in 1965 by a group of private school educators, 39 schools applied for membership in the first year, and a national office was established in Washington, D.C.

Today, NATTS's membership includes more than 850 institutions teaching skills for over 98 careers. As the name indicates, the membership is largely comprised of trade and technical schools, differentiating it from AICS, which largely represents business schools. The curricula of some schools in the two associations overlap a great deal, however. Membership in the associations requires that the school be accredited by the companion accrediting commission. (In addition to these organizations, three national accrediting associations are recognized.)

Proprietary schools after World War II

Several important changes occurred for proprietary schools immediately following World War II, but perhaps none was as important as the passage of the GI Bill. Providing $14 billion in education and job training assistance to nearly 8 million returning veterans, the GI Bill is most frequently remembered as the ticket to undergraduate and graduate education for many ex-servicemen. In fact, however, less than one-third of the total veteran population trained through the GI Bill's provisions attended a college or university. The majority received on-the-job training or farm training, or attended noncollegiate institutions, including proprietary schools (U.S. Congress 1988).

Private career schools participated in the GI Bill under wording in the law that allowed postsecondary schools "approved" by a state to offer training under the GI Bill. Nearly twice as many veterans chose enrollment in a vocational school than in a college or university. According to one author, the result was an explosion in the number of proprietary schools, as evidenced by the growth of GI Bill–approved schools in the 20 years following the war. The number of schools approved during this period rose from just over 3,000 to almost 9,000, with nearly all of the growth attributed to private career schools (Starr 1973, p. 236). And it marked a shift away from what had been private, tuition-supported schools into an era of publicly supported, tuition-assisted programs.

Growth in private career schools was paralleled by increased enrollment in traditional colleges. College enrollment increased 73 percent from 1939 to 1949. The GI Bill enabled veterans to enroll in the school or college of their choice.

Controversy soon surrounded the rapid growth in the number of proprietary schools. Between 1950 and 1952, at least five reports were released by various federal government entities that sharply criticized this growth and the course offerings and quality of education provided by many of the schools. They included reports from the Veterans Administration, the General Accounting Office, and the Bureau of the Budget and two by a special committee established in the House of Representatives to examine abuses of benefits from the GI Bill (McClure 1986).

The Teague Committee, named for its Texas chairman, found that some private career schools billed the government for students never enrolled, falsified cost and attendance information, trained students for careers with few job openings, and committed other abuses of the program's provisions (McClure 1986). Some restrictions were made in program amendments in the 1950s, but they did little to stop the phenomenal growth of the sector.

Another important event in the postwar years occurred a decade later with the passage of the National Vocational Student Loan Insurance (NVSLI) Act of 1965. That act was passed about the same time as the Higher Education Act and included a program of direct lending and federal loan guarantees to students in various types of postsecondary vocational, trade and technical, and business schools. In its report, the House of Representatives argued that the bill was necessary because of the large segment of the population pursuing or interested in pursuing vocational education. Sensitive to the abuses noted by the Teague Committee and others, however, the bill's sponsors carefully noted that it contained provisions intended to prevent such abuses, including the requirement that schools be accredited by a nationally recognized accrediting agency, a state agency recognized by the commissioner of education, or an advisory committee appointed by the commissioner (U.S. Congress 1965).

Nearly twice as many veterans chose enrollment in a vocational school than in a college or university.

For all practical purposes, the NVSLI Act was the same as the guaranteed loan program established for college students under Part B of the Higher Education Act. Congress acknowledged as much when, in the Higher Education Amendments of 1968, the NVSLI program and the Guaranteed Student Loan program of Part B were merged. At the same time, proprietary school students were also made eligible to participate in the College Work Study and National Defense Student Loan programs, though under more restrictive conditions than for college students.

Societal forces played an important role in the postwar growth of private career schools. Two are most prominent. One was the tremendous technological change occurring at the time.

During this period, new products, improved techniques, and more productive methods flowed from the research laboratories and experimental centers, in ever-increasing complexity and in multiple proportions to the funds expended. As a consequence, employment requirements changed (Clark and Sloan 1966, p. 17).

Thus, industry demanded persons skilled in the assembly, repair, and operation of increasingly complicated machines. This new wave of postwar technology was a significant factor in the growth of many trade and technical proprietary schools during the period (p. 17).

The other important change was the evolution and growth of community colleges. As is well known in the history of higher education, community colleges were an extension of the strong emphasis placed on equal educational opportunity following the war. They were seen both as "feeder" institutions for their four-year counterparts and as terminal prebaccalaureate programs for training people in specific job skills. Private career schools were in some ways seen as an alternative to community colleges because less emphasis was placed on general education, frequently allowing a shorter time to complete the program.

Data on the growth of the sector during the postwar period, though limited, show how dramatic the changes were in just two decades. One of the only broad surveys of proprietary schools conducted before the mid-1970s counted some 7,071 private vocational schools in 1966 with an estimated 1.56 million students enrolled (Belitsky 1969). Reported by type of school, the survey showed that more than 800,000 students were enrolled in 3,000 trade and technical schools and another 700,000 were enrolled in about 4,000 business, cosmetology, and barber programs (see table 1).

TABLE 1

ESTIMATED NUMBER OF PROPRIETARY VOCATIONAL SCHOOLS AND STUDENTS IN THE UNITED STATES: 1966

Occupational Category	Number of Schools	Number of Students
Trade and technical	3,000	835,710
Business	1,300	439,500
Cosmetology	2,477	272,470
Barber	294	15,876
Total	**7,071**	**1,563,556**

Source: Belitsky 1969, p. 9.

Notably, in Belitsky's taxonomy of schools, the trade and technical sector accounted for over 50 percent of the total enrollments in proprietary schools. Cosmetology schools, relatively uncommon before the war, accounted for 17 percent of total enrollments, and business schools, the previously dominant segment, made up another 28 percent of total enrollments. Though no directly comparable figures exist for earlier years, both the trade and technical and the cosmetology schools appear to have been major winners in terms of enrollments during the postwar period.

The 1972 Higher Education Act Amendments
Major changes to the Higher Education Act and to the way higher education is financed in the United States were brought about by the 1972 Amendments to the act. The most important was the establishment of the Basic Educational Opportunity Grant (BEOG, later renamed Pell Grant) program, but the amendments also established the Student Loan Marketing Association (Sallie Mae) to provide liquidity to lenders and thereby stimulate students' increased participation in the guaranteed loan program and the "1202" state planning commissions, which were directed to include proprietary schools in state postsecondary education planning.

At the same time, private career schools were made full partners with traditional higher education institutions in the receipt of student aid. The significance of this event lies in the fact that students at proprietary schools would be considered on equal footing with college students in the determination of need and the awarding of federal grants. This event has had a profound effect on both private career schools and traditional higher education institutions (discussed more fully later).

The decision to include proprietary schools in the definition of "eligible institutions" for all aid programs was not reached easily. Interestingly, the dichotomy of opinions currently expressed about private career schools in the public policy arena in many ways closely resembles Congress's "split personality" view of this sector in 1972. The Senate committee report notes that it was in favor of creating benefits for students based on their individual needs, without regard to the type of institution a particular student attended. Yet the same report also notes that it was concerned with the prospect that:

*. . . students attracted by sophisticated advertising and un-
fillable promises may enroll in schools [that] do not offer
the quality of education . . . the schools claim is available.
This is the case particularly with regard to certain technical
occupations, where . . . the students are offered courses of
study for which jobs are unavailable* (McClure 1986, p. 9).

Now, nearly two decades later, almost the precise same
words could be used to describe the sentiments of many who
are currently engaged in public policy debates over proprietary schools' participation in student aid programs.

Comparing Proprietary Career Schools and Traditional Higher Education

Common characteristics

Today's private career schools are frequently compared and
contrasted with traditional higher education institutions on
many levels, and most of this comparison is made by those
who believe that proprietary schools are unworthy participants
in federal student assistance programs. These comparisons
are frequently made to point out differences between the for-
profit and nonprofit sectors and conclude by arguing that for-
profit schools should be served by a separate set of student
aid programs. Yet several commonalities have been noted in
the research that help to bridge the line of demarcation
between the two sectors. These commonalities also help to
explain the character of private career schools and their
methods of operation.

One important similarity between the two sectors is that
they both enroll a significant number of students. According
to one estimate, in 1987 at least 1.4 million students were
enrolled in resident proprietary school programs and an additional 1.5 million students were enrolled in home study
schools (some of which are eligible for federal student aid
funds). Therefore, some 25 percent of full-time equivalent
students enrolled in undergraduate postsecondary education
are in private career schools (Lee 1988a, p. 2).

Another area of similarity between the two sectors concerns
degree-granting status. While over 90 percent of proprietary
schools are limited to granting certificates, an increasing number have become accredited to award associate and higher
degrees. According to an examination of NATTS- and AICS-
accredited schools, more than 270 private career schools grant

associate degrees, 41 grant bachelor's degrees, and 22 offer master's degree programs. Many of these degree-granting schools are also accredited by the regional accrediting organizations typically used by colleges and universities (Lee 1988a, pp. 16–19). Thus, a limited number (an estimated 150) of proprietary schools provide similar education and are subject to the same accreditation standards as nonprofit colleges.

Some overlap also occurs among private career schools and others in the collegiate sector in the education they provide. Indeed, in some instances, traditional colleges contract with proprietary schools to offer specialized vocational training. For example, colleges and universities that have technical programs but do not always have specialized instructors might contract with a private career school to offer training to their students either on or off campus. This arrangement frequently occurs in the case of cosmetology programs.

Some evidence also suggests a significant overlap in students; for example, half the students in proprietary schools attend a college either before or after their enrollment in a private career school (Lee 1990a).

Distinguishing characteristics

The literature on proprietary schools notes several ways in which for-profit schools differ from nonprofit colleges and universities: their management and decision-making methods and the special circumstances faced by the owners and managers of private career schools compared to traditional college administrators. Generalizations about management and administration are difficult because of the range in size and complexity of for-profit schools, from sole proprietors to large, publicly traded corporations.

One important dissimilarity between the profit-making and nonprofit sectors concerns the structure of the decision-making authority. In a proprietary school, the owners or corporate directors are more likely to make critical decisions regarding the direction of the school, financial choices, program mix, and admissions or other academic standards (although some schools in the sector have strongly decentralized decision-making processes). Administrative staff are usually limited to day-to-day management decisions, such as setting course schedules and certifying attendance. In traditional higher education, decision making is diffused among community boards, departments, and other faculty organizations. Generally, different people have the power to make decisions in the two sectors.

Another important difference between the two sectors is that the decision-making process is guided by different considerations. Private school owners must, by the nature of the enterprise, focus decision making on profitability, particularly with respect to issues like facilities, course selection, and faculty compensation and benefits. Nonprofit colleges and universities are motivated by somewhat different factors. In particular, colleges and universities tend to have to respond to various constituents—boards of trustees, academic departments, the tenured faculty, and so on. With the exception of chain schools with elaborate corporate structures, proprietary schools have fewer concerns with these layers of constituents in their decision making. Thus, in some ways, the private career school benefits from a streamlined decision-making process compared to traditional colleges.

Which is not to say that nonprofit private and public colleges totally disregard constraints on income and efforts to control costs. Enrollment is directly related to income in both public and private colleges, and traditional colleges have become increasingly active in marketing their programs to potential students in response to a shrinking market. Colleges modify their course offerings to meet students' and employers' needs as well as changes in the context of the discipline. The growth of enrollments in business curricula is an example of a response to market needs.

Boards of trustees play a much larger role in public and nonprofit colleges than in private career schools. Proprietary schools often have advisory boards, but they lack the far-reaching legal responsibilities of traditional collegiate boards of trustees. (It is beyond the scope of this report to determine how well boards actually improve colleges' public accountability.)

One important issue raised in the literature and in public policy discussions is whether the profit motive has an effect on meeting the needs of students and the community. Put differently, does the search for profitability in the proprietary sector result in serving the public interest more or less effectively than in the nonprofit sector? This question is difficult to answer, because in some ways, the goals of the two types of schools are different. "Private schools are rooted in the marketplace and survive only if their income from students exceeds their training expenses" (Wilms 1976, p. 171).

This argument suggests that, using some carefully defined measure of "success," proprietary schools should do a better job than other schools in preparing students who are ultimately successful in the labor market. Nonprofit institutions tend to rely on other measures of students' success—enrollment in graduate school, public confidence in the reputation of the school, and even political gains (in terms of increased funding) in the case of public, nonprofit institutions.

By the narrow measure of graduation and job placement rates, one analysis concludes that graduates of private schools had about the same success in the labor market as others (Wilms 1976), which is consistent with results reported in a more detailed discussion of the broader concerns about outcomes of proprietary education (see the next section). Because the missions differ, traditional education is not as easily defined in terms of institutional completion rates and success in the employment market.

Private career schools and the nonprofit sectors also differ in what might be called the traditions of postsecondary education. The day-to-day environment at a proprietary school is considerably removed from the environment at a typical college or university. Several examples come to mind. The lack of tenure for teachers, for instance, means more faculty turnover. Likewise, the nontraditional calendar at a private career school—rolling admissions, with programs beginning frequently—varies from the normal semester system at many colleges and universities and rarely includes long holiday breaks or summer vacations (though these traditions would appear to be changing at colleges and universities with the growth in enrollments of nontraditional students).[3] The limited decision-making role of faculty at proprietary schools also contrasts with the shared authority faculty members exercise in the collegiate sector. Even facilities can differ. Private career schools often use leased space located close to students, and they do not include the same emphasis on sports or auxiliary facilities, such as housing, health facilities, or food concessions, usually found in colleges.

---

3. For a general discussion of school operation and attendance schedules, see, e.g., Belitsky 1969, pp. 36–38.

Curricula

Private career schools offer students diverse curricula, not because most schools offer a wide range of programs, but because of the large number of special-purpose schools and the rapidity with which schools can change their course selection to respond to the market or to local employers' requests. Most private career schools specialize in one or two fields.

The diversity of programs offered by proprietary schools makes it difficult to generalize. Programs can vary from sophisticated, high-tech training courses to entry-level training. Several common threads run through these programs, however, that can help to describe the curricula of private career schools in general terms.

Most proprietary school programs are designed to develop specific job skills. This important characteristic distinguishes most for-profit programs from their nonprofit counterparts, which propose to educate the "whole person." The research in this area shows that most private school programs de-emphasize broader educational goals (beyond basic skills in literacy needed to do the job) and focus on the specifics of the occupation, including behavior in the workplace and employers' expectations.

The typical program in a proprietary school organizes courses into sequential units, each of which covers a discrete topic. Each segment might last a specific period of time. For example, a cosmetology course of 1,200 hours would probably be organized into a dozen or more instructional units, with each unit covering a specific skill necessary for the student to become a practicing cosmetologist. The unit on permanent waves, for example, might be 100 hours, manicures and pedicures 150, and hairstyling as much as 200. These units are viewed as independent, distinct segments that the student should learn before proceeding to the next phase.

Further, private career school programs have few, if any, options in the curriculum. All students in the same program usually take the same courses in identical sequence. Thus, they have little variability in the selection of courses or their timing. In fact, because many proprietary school programs are geared toward learning a skill that ultimately requires local or state certification and licensing—truck driving or x-ray technician, for example—programs cannot vary from a prescribed course in a specific order. Thus, private career schools place less emphasis on extracurricular programs compared to colleges and universities.

The courses of study at private trade schools vary in length. For example, in 1987 the programs at schools accredited by NATTS varied from eight weeks to 152 weeks (Lee 1987, p. 26). Programs at cosmetology schools typically require 1,000 hours of classroom and practical instruction (at least six months in actual duration), and some last 1,500 hours or more. Technical business programs, commercial art, and electronics are all examples of those lasting longer than one year.

The tremendous variation in the types of programs offered at proprietary schools makes generalizations tenuous at best. In addition to Belitsky's previously noted categories of trade and technical, business, cosmetology, and barber (1969, p. 9), other authors have used more complicated schemes to classify schools (see, e.g., Clark and Sloan 1966, p. 17). Regardless of the taxonomy used, however, none are truly comprehensive. The tremendous range in the types of schools and the new programs being developed each year will probably always hinder any simple universal classification system. Attempts are under way, however, to use the U.S. Department of Education's Classification of Instructional Programs (CIP) to standardize program classification (Lee 1990b).

In the field of public policy, the most common classification of programs is roughly the same as the membership of the major accrediting organizations and associations. Thus, many classify private career schools as trade and technical, business, cosmetology, home study, health, and "other." Following this taxonomy probably accounts for nearly all of the accredited proprietary schools of most immediate interest to policy makers.

Further, private career schools have few, if any, options in the curriculum.

This taxonomy lists the general areas in which students can obtain training from a private career school. The specific programs in which students can enroll are as diverse as the students themselves. As just one example, consider the trade and technical schools as one subset of the proprietary sector. Within this subset, students can be trained in a variety of major programs, from barbering to allied health to auto mechanics. Students can also be enrolled in less known programs, such as horseshoeing, engraving, and photography.

Table 2 lists the types of programs offered at the 544 trade and technical schools Belitsky studied to show more com-

TABLE 2

PROGRAMS OFFERED AT TRADE AND TECHNICAL SCHOOLS

Program	Number of Courses Available in Each Program Area
Auto maintenance and related services	127
Commercial arts	61
Construction	41
Data processing	185
Drafting	131
Drycleaning and laundry	10
Electronics	159
Fashion design, needle trades, and shoemaking	63
Floristry and groundskeeping	14
Food preparation, processing, service, and merchandising	25
Funeral work	6
Hotel/motel operation	12
Industrial management	7
Interior design and related services	21
Investigation	3
Jewelry design and repair	13
Machine shop	30
Major and minor appliance repair and servicing	53
Medical services	154
Performing arts	8
Personal services	9
Photography	18
Printing	27
Radio-TV	95
Recreation and sports	8
Sales, promotions, and related services	21
Tool and die design	54
Transportation–Air	47
Transportation–Freight	6
Transportation–Highway	7
Transportation–Sea	11
Transportation–Space	2
Transportation–Traffic management	9
Waste reconversion	1
Welding	54

Source: Belitsky 1969, pp. 16–24.

pletely the diversity of programs offered at different private career schools. It lists major program areas and the number of possible courses that could be taken in each. AS the table shows, diversity is present not only in the types of programs offered (from auto maintenance to drafting to interior design) but also in the level of specialty within each type of program.

Size and location

As diverse as the curricula are at proprietary schools in this country, relative enrollments per school and their locations are equally diverse—another contrast with the nonprofit sector.

According to the most recent estimate of enrollments in accredited private career schools, proprietary school institutions vary from four students to more than 6,000 on any one campus. The average enrollment at these schools in 1987 was 378, the modal enrollment slightly over 100 (Lee 1988a, p. 7). Thus, according to these figures, the typical private career school is considerably smaller than a traditional college. Average enrollment in traditional colleges in 1985 was nearly 4,000, and the enrollment for at least one campus exceeded 60,000 students (U.S. Dept. of Education 1988, p. 162).

The estimate of the size of schools in this study is less reliable than one would hope for several reasons. First, the numbers used to calculate the enrollment figures are based on reports from the three major accrediting agencies—AICS, NACCAS, and NATTS. Thus, the survey includes only accredited schools, probably accounting for no more than two-thirds of the total universe of residential private schools.[4] Second, the study notes that considerable underreporting of enrollments is endemic to the industry. And third, for reasons related to the method in which the accrediting agency collects information about enrollments, the numbers for cosmetology schools can only be estimated.

Despite these limitations, the report does provide the best and most current available information on enrollments in accredited proprietary schools. Because accreditation is

---

4. This figure is based on estimates that by now are becoming dated. A federal government survey in 1982 counted 6,013 private career schools, which does not include home study schools (discussed later in this section). See U.S. Dept. of Education 1982, p. xiv.

Proprietary Schools

TABLE 3

AICS-, NATTS-, and NACCAS-ACCREDITED SCHOOLS, BY STATE: 1987

State	Enrollment	Number of Institutions
New York	191,014	238
California	163,124	530
Ohio	79,658	196
Illinois	75,280	196
Texas	74,198	257
Pennsylvania	73,597	216
Puerto Rico	68,582	111
Florida	57,161	191
New Jersey	44,858	117
Missouri	40,792	106
Arizona	36,647	95
Louisiana	34,899	95
Michigan	33,655	138
Colorado	27,749	78
Georgia	27,191	54
Indiana	22,366	91
Maryland	21,757	47
Tennessee	20,649	75
Virginia	20,242	69
Massachusetts	19,950	73
Connecticut	18,792	58
Minnesota	18,314	58
Kentucky	18,082	55
Rhode Island	16,366	23
Washington	16,209	69
Oklahoma	15,862	59
Alabama	15,499	42
Wisconsin	11,396	38
North Carolina	11,066	40
South Carolina	9,939	39
Oregon	9,303	54
New Hampshire	8,907	17
Kansas	8,195	40
Arkansas	7,814	35
Mississippi	7,509	36
Washington, D.C.	7,299	19
Nevada	6,342	27
Iowa	5,998	44
West Virginia	5,463	19
South Dakota	5,136	9
Utah	4,942	38

TABLE 3 (continued)

**AICS-, NATTS-, and NACCAS-ACCREDITED SCHOOLS,
BY STATE: 1987**

State	Enrollment	Number of Institutions
Nebraska	4,902	29
Maine	4,114	19
New Mexico	3,239	26
North Dakota	2,777	14
Hawaii	2,350	9
Wyoming	2,318	7
Delaware	1,774	10
Idaho	1,195	13
Guam	617	1
Vermont	570	5
Montana	530	14
Alaska	404	2
Non-U.S.	3,572	8
Total	**1,390,164**	**3,949**

Source: Lee 1988a, pp. 10,11.

believed to be the major "gatekeeper" for the receipt of federal student aid funds, the information available on these schools is important for setting public policy.

Table 3 shows that the total enrollment in accredited private career schools in 1987 was 1,390,164, based on a total universe of 3,949 accredited schools. The enrollment by state shows that the top five states—New York, California, Ohio, Illinois, and Texas—accounted for over 40 percent of the total enrollment in accredited proprietary schools. In fact, New York and California alone make up one-quarter of the total enrollments in accredited private schools.

Further data on the geographic location of proprietary schools are also revealing. For example, private career schools are more likely to be located in urban areas than traditional colleges and universities.[5] Most proprietary schools do not offer student housing, and, because of frequently limited student income, the convenience of the location of the campus is an important consideration. The desire to live at home is

------

5. For a thorough examination of the issues concerning these urban schools, see Hyde 1976.

an important factor influencing the choice to attend a private career school (Friedlander 1980, p. 33). Most likely, school owners are aware of this phenomenon and seek to locate schools in advantageous locations.

One important aspect concerning the size and location of proprietary schools relates to the subset of home study schools in the private sector. These schools are distinctive, and a few points about them are worth mentioning here.[6] Because some correspondence programs are currently eligible for federal student loan funds, information on accredited home study schools would be helpful in rounding out the definition of for-profit trade schools.

Approximately 1.5 million students participate in home study programs accredited by the National Home Study Council. This enrollment is limited to only about 60 institutions, suggesting that the concentration of students in these schools must be significant in some cases (Lee 1988a). Only 22 of these schools are qualified for federal student aid. Roughly 100,000 home study school students participate in the Stafford Loan program. Indeed, according to unpublished data from the U.S. Department of Education, some of the largest institutional recipients of federal student loan funds are home study schools. One correspondence school alone accounted for over $100 million in federally guaranteed student loans in 1988. Hence, these schools should be examined more thoroughly in future studies concerned with public policy.

Staffing and pay

The literature on private career schools contains comparatively little information about instructional and administrative staff and compensation, because few large-scale surveys have been conducted in this area and those that have tend to collect information on the characteristics of students and their perceptions. While some general studies have been done of the characteristics of teachers in vocational programs (see, e.g., Evelyn 1971), none the authors are aware of focus specifically on instructors at proprietary schools.

Perhaps the most thorough examination of proprietary school staffing and pay, however, was completed in 1972. This

---

6. Several volumes concern home study schools; see, e.g., Noffsinger 1926 and MacKenzie et al. 1968 for excellent historical treatments of these schools.

study found that most teachers at private career schools were hired from industry. In fact, many were also found to be employed concurrently in a field similar to the one they were teaching (Wolman et al. 1972). Proprietary school instructors also tend to be younger than faculty at public vocational institutions (Wolman et al. 1972). Few are required to have a college degree, and many fields of instruction require no state certification or license. The exceptions are in the degree-granting institutions, where faculty education is often comparable to that in public and private colleges. Instructors are more likely to work a standard year instead of a nine-month academic year. Few have special job security or contract assurances comparable to tenure in the nonprofit sector. And teachers tend to be less well paid than instructors at public vocational schools.[7]

Administrative staff serve a different function at private career schools than at public vocational schools or other nonprofit colleges and universities for several reasons. First, few proprietary schools have housing or other facilities for maintaining students on campus (although most help to arrange private housing for students who need it). Therefore, few administrators are concerned with student housing, dining facilities, counseling, or health services. Second, most private career schools do not have extensive libraries or other academic support facilities and thus do not have to staff them. Third, proprietary schools concentrate more on recruitment, completing the program, and job placement. At smaller schools, one person might serve several of these functions.

Students' characteristics

A number of studies about private career schools conducted in the last two decades examine students' characteristics. The purpose of Belitsky's study (1969) was to determine the extent to which proprietary schools could be used in the training of disadvantaged students; its results are particularly telling in establishing current public policy (although the results concerning students' socioeconomic and other characteristics are based on questionnaires sent to NATTS schools only).

The average age of students was approximately 20, and more than 10 percent of all students were over the age of 26.

---

7. For a discussion of the role of instructors in the overall proprietary school environment, see Belitsky 1969.

Grouping the students into two categories, however—those enrolled in day sessions and those enrolled in night sessions—led to the finding that nearly 40 percent of the evening students were older than 26, leading to the conclusion that a significant percentage of day students likely did not have full-time work experience but that many of the evening students were working or had worked full-time at some point (Belitsky 1969).

Of those enrolled in the NATTS schools surveyed, men were more commonly enrolled than women. In fact, about two-thirds of the schools had enrollments that were at least 90 percent male. (The study unfortunately did not examine the racial or ethnic characteristics of these students.)

Much of the financial information gathered is now irrelevant because of many private career schools' current reliance on federal student aid. Interestingly, even in the late 1960s, few students reported relying on parental support to finance their training. Sixty-six percent of the schools reported that some of their students received loans, either from banks or directly from the institution (Belitsky 1969).

Findings on dropouts are also telling. Somewhat surprisingly, the median dropout rate for day classes was 14 percent and for evening classes was 20 percent—low figures even by 1960s standards. Respondents cited financial problems as the main reason for dropping out, followed by personal or family problems.

An analysis of the characteristics of some 1,370 proprietary students and 2,270 graduates from 50 randomly selected public vocational programs and private career schools in four metropolitan areas found that those attending proprietary schools generally "brought fewer resources to school" with them, compared to vocational students attending community colleges (Wilms 1976). In contrast to those attending vocational programs at community colleges or technical institutes, private school students were more likely to be high school dropouts or graduates of high school vocational programs (Wilms 1976). The students who attended and graduated from proprietary schools tended to have weaker verbal skills and were more often from ethnic minority groups.

Especially intriguing was the finding that minority and other disadvantaged students preferred private career schools even over nearby public institutions offering the same training at a fraction of the cost (Wilms 1976), leading Wilms to speculate that it might have been because public postsecondary schools were perceived to be an extension of the academic middle-class public secondary school system and therefore not attractive to many of these students. No discernible difference was found in the motivation, goal orientation, or ego development of public versus proprietary school students.

Other data suggest that private career school students' reasons for attending their schools differ from those who attend community colleges. The top-ranked reasons given by students attending private career schools were reputation, availability of desired courses, financial aid, and job placement rates. Community college students also note desired courses as an important reason for enrolling, but lower tuition, ability to attend school while working, and living at home were given a high rank (Apling and Aleman 1990).

A survey of 10,000 NATTS students found a high level of satisfaction with the school:

- 89 percent were satisfied with their courses;
- 87 percent were satisfied with their teachers;
- 80 percent would recommend the school to a friend (Downes 1991).

On a scale of one (totally satisfied) to five (not satisfied), the students responded as follows:

Rating	Percent
1	26
2	40
3	23
4	7
5	3

A pilot study for the Higher Education Research Institute (Christian 1975) also developed some interesting findings about students' characteristics. This study, which included only those attending accredited proprietary schools, found that they came from lower socioeconomic backgrounds than traditional college students. It also found that private career school students differed from traditional college students in terms of demographics and background, with proprietary students more likely to be female, older, married, and African-American.

Two interesting findings related to finances arose from this study. First, offers of financial assistance were a very important factor in a student's decision to attend a private career school. Second, a higher proportion of proprietary students participated in federal student aid programs than in other sectors.

Perhaps the most extensive study of students' characteristics at private career schools is a survey of 3,020 students at schools accredited by NATTS or AICS (Friedlander 1980). The main purpose of the study was descriptive: to find out who enrolls in proprietary schools, what types of programs are attractive to them, what their motivations are for attending, and how they pay for their training. A comparison sample of 2,626 community college students was also surveyed.

Private career school students tend to be older than their full-time community college counterparts and are more likely to have been away from high school for a time (Friedlander 1980). A considerable proportion (more than 30 percent) had attended other postsecondary institutions. In fact, some had already obtained a degree at another type of institution.

Proprietary schools also enroll larger percentages of women and minorities than community colleges (Friedlander 1980). By accrediting agency, AICS-accredited schools tended to enroll a higher proportion of women, NATTS schools a higher proportion of minorities. Private career school students come from lower income levels than their community college counterparts and have parents who have achieved lower levels of formal education.

Findings regarding academic preparation are inconclusive. For example, one study found that more than half of all proprietary school students were enrolled in college preparatory programs in high school but notes that lower proportions of private career school students than community college students completed college preparatory courses (Friedlander 1980). A summary of Friedlander's more important findings about students' characteristics is found in table 4.

The few studies that have been conducted since 1980 to collect detailed information on the characteristics of proprietary school students confirm earlier findings. For example, private career school students were more likely to have enrolled in a vocational or general curriculum program in high school compared to those going to college (Laoria 1984). Proprietary school students also received slightly lower grades in high school compared to their academic peers (Laoria 1984).

TABLE 4

CHARACTERISTICS OF NATTS AND
AICS STUDENTS COMPARED TO
COMMUNITY COLLEGE STUDENTS: 1980

	Proprietary Schools (percent)	Community Colleges (percent)
Gender		
Female	66	48
Male	34	52
Age		
Under 19	35	72
19 to 21	35	23
22 and over	30	5
Race		
African-American	24	6
White	68	87
Other	8	7
Family Income		
Under $8,000	32	19
$8,000 to $15,000	34	37
$15,000 to $20,000	12	19
$20,000 and over	23	26
High School Grades		
A	9	9
B+ to B	41	42
B– to C+	31	35
C– to D	18	15
High School Achievement		
High school graduate	89	98
Nongraduate, GED	6	1
No degree	5	1

Source: Friedlander 1980, pp. 16, 19, 20, 24, 25.

The most current findings concerning the characteristics
of students attending private career schools come from the
1987 National Postsecondary Student Aid Study (NPSAS) (U.S.
Dept. of Education 1987). NPSAS collected data on an autumn

TABLE 5

CHARACTERISTICS OF PROPRIETARY SCHOOL STUDENTS: 1987 NPSAS

Students in Private Career Schools	(percent)
Age	
Under 24	54
24 to 29	21
30 and over	25
Race/Ethnicity	
American Indian	1
Asian or Pacific Islander	3
African-American	21
Hispanic	14
White	60
Other	1
Income	
Under $11,000	47
$11,000 to $22,999	23
$23,000 and over	26
Unknown	5

Source: U.S. Dept. of Education 1987.

1986 national sample of students and included responses from parents, institutional registrars, and student financial aid officers. Data from the survey are presented in table 5.

The average age of proprietary school students is 24, slightly older than students entering traditional colleges. This sector also enrolls a significant percentage of minority students and low-income students. Nearly half of private career school students have incomes below $11,000 (which includes both dependent and independent students). Eighty-four percent of private career school students attend full time, compared to 62 percent for students who attend other types of schools. Proprietary school students are more frequently enrolled in a high school vocational program and of lower tested ability than college students. Nearly identical percentages (55 percent) live at home with their parents while attending private career schools or traditional colleges (Korb et al. 1988).

In general, then, studies on characteristics of students at proprietary schools have found them more likely to be low income, female, and members of a minority group compared to traditional college students. Private career school students tend to be older than full-time undergraduate students in colleges or universities but younger than community college students and are also more likely to be financially independent. Proprietary school students tend to score lower in academic ability than other students and are more likely to have taken a vocational program in high school. (These averages do not take into consideration the difference among students enrolled in different programs.)[8]

One of the most important factors associated with enrollment would appear to be the gender of students. For example, according to one survey (U.S. Dept. of Education 1982), the business, cosmetology, and health fields accounted for more than 70 percent of private career school enrollments by women, while the trade and technical fields accounted for more than 60 percent of male enrollments.

More than half (54 percent) of all students in proprietary schools in one study majored in a business or secretarial field (Friedlander 1980). Approximately 17 percent majored in one of the trade and technical fields. By occupational preference, the most popular jobs were clerical (30 percent), business (20 percent), and trade and technical (15 percent) (Friedlander 1980, p. 39), although this mix of programs may have changed since the survey was done.

A study of 561 NATTS schools found that the most popular fields of study (in terms of enrollments) in trade and technical schools were air conditioning, refrigeration, and heating; allied health; electronics technology; and auto/diesel mechanics (Greenberg and Torabi 1985). These programs are among more than 100 major fields of study found at NATTS-accredited schools. A more recent (1988) analysis by the authors of unpublished data from NATTS-accredited schools found similar results. As table 6 shows, allied health, truck driving, and skills for electricians have the largest enrollments. Notably, air conditioning, refrigeration, and heating appears much farther down the list when compared to the earlier survey (probably partly because the NATTS survey accounts for only about one-third of the total enrollment in NATTS-accredited schools, which may bias the results).

One of the most important factors associated with enrollment would appear to be the gender of students.

---

8. Students enrolled in degree-granting schools are similar to those in not-for-profit and public colleges.

TABLE 6

ANNUAL ENROLLMENT IN NATTS-ACCREDITED SCHOOLS, BY TYPE OF SCHOOL: 1988

Type of Program	Enrollment	Percent of Total
Allied health	50,774	9.7
Truck driver	33,177	6.3
Electrician	19,557	3.7
Automotive/small engine/diesel	17,733	3.4
Computer	12,878	2.5
Word processing/data entry/ secretary	7,368	1.4
Aviation	6,732	1.3
Travel	6,525	1.2
Photography/printing	6,070	1.2
Barber	5,519	1.1
Food service/culinary	4,011	0.8
Welding	3,540	0.7
Fashion design/merchandising	2,004	0.4
Drafting/interior design	1,932	0.4
Air conditioning/refrigeration/ heating	1,752	0.3
Broadcasting	1,572	0.3
Total	181,144	34.6
Other programs	342,648	65.4
Total All Programs	**523,792**	**100.0**

Source: Unpublished NATTS data 1988.

Information on the types of programs students are taking at AICS-accredited schools is also available. Enrollment numbers for AICS programs are based on information provided by students taking the Career Programs Assessment test (CPAt), administered by the American College Testing program. The test measures entry-level skills of students in postsecondary institutions offering occupational programs. In 1988, over 66,000 students enrolled in 243 AICS member schools were tested.

Regrettably, these data have problems as well. The sample of students is not representative and might reflect the schools with an interest in having students take the CPAt rather than any measure of a program's popularity. Further, nearly one-third of the students tested did not enter a valid program code on the test form. Nevertheless, the information provides some sense of the programs with the greatest enrollment. In rank order of greatest enrollment, the top 20 programs in AICS schools were word processing equipment operator, accountant, secretary, data typist, medical assistant, nursing assistant, computer operator, data processor, business administration, travel/tourism management, computer programmer, office manager/assistant, receptionist, security officer, engineering technician, legal/paralegal assistant, electronics technology, legal secretary, bookkeeper, and medical secretary. While this information is helpful in describing the types of programs students are taking by accrediting agency, it provides little insight about the overall popularity of programs in the whole private career school sector. Unfortunately, no comprehensive information is available on this subject, again hampering meaningful decision making based on reliable information about proprietary schools.

Interestingly, the 1987 NPSAS does provide some information on the type of program in which students were enrolled. Unfortunately, the NPSAS data are handicapped by several problems. They underrepresent enrollment in private career schools, because the survey is a "snapshot" and only includes fall enrollees (therefore not capturing the rolling admissions cycle of proprietary schools). Further, NPSAS was not conceived to provide information about enrollments by program and sector, and therefore some sampling bias likely exists. Thus, these results cannot be reported here.

Nevertheless, NPSAS provides another point useful in defining enrollment in the private career school sector. Because the information was categorized with the CIP code used by the Department of Education, a precedent has been set in the collection of future information regarding the enrollment of proprietary school students by program. Any future studies or surveys, including those done by the Department of Education or the associations and accrediting commissions, would benefit from adherence to this coding system. Results would be uniform with those in other postsecondary fields, thus allowing for accurate comparisons, and would lend credibility to the information collected.

OUTCOMES

What do we know about the quality of private career school education? In many ways, the short answer to the question is the same as that to the questions about the demographics and socioeconomic status of proprietary school students: not enough. While much of the public policy discussion about private career schools over the last two decades has been about outcomes, little credible research has been accomplished, partly because the federal government and many states have poor mechanisms for collecting data and disseminating information when it comes to proprietary schools. But a certain amount of responsibility must be placed on the schools themselves, which are at times reluctant to supply such information. Likewise, the major national associations and accrediting bodies do not have detailed information on the rates of program completion or economic outcomes of students in member schools. This lack of information needs to be remedied, given the importance of this debate.

The increasing concern with outcomes is evident in recent congressional interest in graduation and placement rates among all vocational postsecondary schools. In addition, a study of how best to report traditional college completion rates has been mandated. Further, many state and private organizations have become interested in assessing higher education.

What we do know about outcomes for private career school education is fragmentary. It frequently comes from fairly small or incomplete samples of students and graduates. And the data collected in this area often were compiled for other purposes; that is, the outcomes of proprietary school education are usually incidental to some other broad research question under investigation in a particular study. Thus, some caution should be applied in viewing these numbers and interpreting their significance.

Completion Rates

When considering educational outcomes, two basic questions are usually asked. First, did the student complete the program of study satisfactorily? And second, what happened to him or her after graduation? This subsection is concerned primarily with the data that can be brought to bear on the first question.

As many educational researchers know, it is very difficult to obtain information from students who have failed, be they dropouts, "stopouts" who never return, or loan defaulters.

Part of the reason is that many students simply cannot be located; NPSAS found this fact to be especially true for students who defaulted on loans. The other part of the reason is a student's unwillingness to participate in a survey that is linked to his or her educational failure. Thus, caution is urged to those who wish to attach major importance to data in this area.

One of the better sources of information on completion in the modern era of private career school training—since the 1972 Education Amendments—is the biannual surveys of postsecondary schools with occupational programs conducted by the National Center for Education Statistics. Data from the 1978 survey show that 63 percent of proprietary school students were reported (by school administrators) to have completed their programs of study, compared to 46 percent in public vocational institutions (Jung 1980, pp. 18–20). Another 7 percent of the private career school students and 9 percent of the public postsecondary school attendees were classified as "leavers"—students who did not graduate but were deemed by the school to have sufficient skills to obtain a job. Thus, close to 30 percent of the proprietary school students and 45 percent of the public vocational school students were classified as dropouts.

These results should be viewed with caution, however. Unknown reporting errors on the part of school administrators may have had some effect on findings. Further, because many public and some private vocational school programs allow students to earn academic credits that can be transferred to degree-granting programs, some of the dropouts might in fact be students who transferred to a traditional college or university.

The sources of data that provide the most comprehensive information on the completion rates of proprietary school students are the two main postsecondary longitudinal studies conducted by the U.S. Department of Education in the last two decades: the National Longitudinal Survey of the Class of 1972 (NLS-72) and the High School and Beyond Survey of the Class of 1980 (HS&B). Both surveys include important data on outcomes for private career school and other postsecondary vocational students but are severely hampered by fairly small numbers of proprietary school students. The data are generally acceptable for use on entire populations of students (e.g., all private career school students) but are probably unacceptable for analyses of subpopulations (e.g., African-American proprietary school students).

The National Assessment of Vocational Education (NAVE), a project of the U.S. Department of Education implemented in January 1987 and completed in late 1989, relied extensively on the HS&B and NLS-72 data bases. It looked at both educational aspirations and attainment to measure outcomes relative to completion. The study found, through an analysis of students who enrolled in less than baccalaureate institutions after high school graduation, that more than 90 percent aspired to obtain a college degree or certificate. Thus, program completion is a more reasonable measure of their educational attainment.

As table 7 shows, the HS&B data indicate that roughly equal percentages of students at public technical institutes and private career schools completed their programs of study—about twice the level of students in community colleges. Of course, a significantly higher percentage of community college students transfers to another postsecondary institution or never intends to obtain a credential. Still, compared to the 1972 high school class, completion rates for the 1980 high school class appear to have remained the same for proprietary schools, increased for public technical institutes (11 percent), but dropped considerably for community colleges (17 percent). NAVE concludes that these data show "a pattern of declining achievement" for community college students (Goodwin 1989, p. 46).

Table 7 also shows that the rates at which students leave school (for the class of 1980) are quite high. About equal percentages of private career school and community college students (42 percent) leave without a degree or certificate, with slightly higher levels for public technical school students (47 percent). In each case, it represents an increase in noncompletion rates compared to the NLS-72 group, with proprietary school students exhibiting the smallest increase in noncompletion. In an analysis not contained in this table, NAVE notes that at community colleges, where students may be enrolled in either academic or vocational programs, no significant differences exist in rates of noncompletion. Thus, the fact that students are in vocational courses appears to have little impact on completion.

These NAVE data should be interpreted carefully for three reasons. First, as already noted, the small number of private

TABLE 7

COMPLETION AND NONCOMPLETION AMONG STUDENTS ENTERING LESS THAN BACCALAUREATE INSTITUTIONS

Outcome	Community Colleges (percent)	Public Technical Institutes (percent)	Proprietary Schools (percent)
Total Completions			
High school class of 1980	19.1	36.1	36.1
High school class of 1972	23.0	32.5	38.5
Left without Credential			
High school class of 1980	42.0	46.5	42.2
High school class of 1972	30.0	35.8	40.5
Transferred to Another Institution			
High school class of 1980	25.2	8.6	13.2
High school class of 1972	28.2	17.8	16.0
Still Enrolled in First School			
High school class of 1980	13.8	9.0	14.0
High school class of 1972	19.9	14.0	5.0

Source: Goodwin 1989, p. 46.

career school students included in both surveys suggests some limitations to the sample. Second, the HS&B data NAVE used include only students in the high school class of 1980; thus, adult students are not part of the study. Because, as previously noted, a significant percentage of students attending proprietary schools is older than their collegiate counterparts, an important group within the private career school population is excluded from the sector. And third, the HS&B data on outcomes are based on a four-year time frame (1980 to 1984) for students who entered a postsecondary program soon after graduating. Therefore, some students who take longer to complete their schooling because of part-time or intermittent enrollment, especially in the community college sector, may not be accurately accounted for in this study.

An examination of the HS&B data base also produced evidence on the completion rates of proprietary school students (see Sango-Jordan 1989), using a broader sample of students, including 1980–81 through 1982–83 enrollments rather than the "immediate enrollees" used by NAVE. It also tracks students for a longer period of time, using data from the third follow-up survey in 1986. The study found that 61 percent of the private career school students had achieved a post-secondary credential by February 1986, compared to 58 percent for students enrolled in four-year programs and 43 percent for those enrolled in "other," less than four-year schools—essentially a variable combining the community college and public technical institute categories (as defined in the NAVE study) with junior college enrollees.

This report also differs from the NAVE report in that it credits a degree or certificate obtained at schools attended after the initial school of enrollment. A community college student receiving a bachelor's degree is credited as a success for the community college. The latter report also differs in its treatment of continuing students who were not included in the equation for completion or noncompletion.

In comparing these results, the reader should keep in mind that students in proprietary schools are more likely to complete a certificate that takes less than one year. Community college students are more likely to finish a two- or four-year degree program to be considered as a successful completer. Thus, the two are not directly comparable. Nevertheless, these results suggest private career schools may do a far better job at limiting dropouts than was previously believed (see "ACE Chief" 1989).

The HS&B data do not provide a complete picture of student outcomes in either the proprietary school or community college sector because the data are limited to a narrow age group. Unfortunately, the nation lacks a comprehensive study of what happens to students as they flow through the education system and into the labor force.

Economic and Employment Outcomes
Once students complete their program of study at a private career school, they presumably enter the job market in search of employment. Because the goal of the training is to acquire marketable skills, this assumption is reasonable. The "success" of the training therefore can be measured through an examination of various economic and employment outcomes following graduation.

Many ways can be used to measure success in terms of employment and economic factors. Researchers have grappled with this problem and have used several different approaches for capturing labor market outcomes. The most obvious is job placement: Did the student leave the school and, within a reasonable amount of time, get a job? Other questions about these outcomes have also been asked. Was the job in the same field as that for which the student was trained? Was the student satisfied with the training or job? What wages did the graduate earn upon entering the work force and at some later time? Unfortunately, these questions are complex, and few answers can be offered confidently.

One of the best early efforts (Wilms 1976) surveyed and interviewed some 2,300 graduates of public community colleges and proprietary schools enrolled in six occupational programs: accounting, computer programming, electronics technology, dental assistance, secretarial, and cosmetology. Questions covered topics such as employment history, earnings, job satisfaction, and postsecondary training satisfaction. Several of the findings are noteworthy.

The study found that in four of the six occupations studied, public vocational school students were significantly more satisfied with their training than the students who had attended private career schools. It also found that a significantly lower percentage of proprietary school graduates (65 percent) than public graduates (90 percent) said they would repeat their choice of school if given a second chance. No statistically significant difference in the earnings of private career versus public school graduates was found, both in terms of first earnings (what they earned soon after graduating) and most recent earnings (survey participants had graduated anywhere from one to three years earlier).

Another study conducted in the 1970s also examined postsecondary vocational graduates' satisfaction with their training (Wolman et al. 1972). This study of graduates in four types of programs (office, health, data processing, and technical) in four cities found that nearly 60 percent of the employed nonprivate career school graduates expressed satisfaction with their training. Only 33 percent of the employed proprietary school graduates expressed similar satisfaction.

A study of proprietary schools in New York City during the 1986–87 academic year found that of the 35 percent of students who completed their programs of study, about 64 percent found work in a field related to their training. The authors concluded that only 22 percent of students who enroll in New York City private career schools eventually find work in the area in which they were enrolled (Banerjee, Zhou, and

Caruso 1989). The data, taken from self-reported, unaudited information compiled by the state education department, are haphazardly reported in this study, and therefore no assessment of their reliability is possible.

The NAVE and Sango-Jordan studies cited earlier are the most recent and comprehensive in terms of economic and employment outcomes. The NAVE study looked at these outcomes from several perspectives, the two most relevant being incidence of unemployment and wage levels.

Using the HS&B data set, NAVE found that type of institution is related to the average incidence of unemployment.[9] Unemployment was defined as a period the student was not working during the previous year, from March 1985 to February 1986. The reason for unemployment could be one of several; for example, absence from the labor market could be the result of having a child or wanting a job but not having one. The study found that the unadjusted incidence of unemployment was 12.7 percent for students who studied at public technical institutes, 17 percent for those at community colleges, and 26.3 percent for those at proprietary schools. The regression-adjusted means of unemployment were similar to the unadjusted means: 16.5 percent for public technical institute trainees, 18.9 percent for community college trainees, and 27.7 percent for private career school trainees.

NAVE also looked briefly at the hourly earnings of students who were employed in February 1986. It found that the unadjusted mean wage per hour was $8.59 for proprietary school graduates, $7.03 for community college graduates, and $6.74 for public technical institute graduates. The model included students' characteristics and amount of time involved in the program. Using the regression adjustment, however, yielded no statistically significant difference in the wages received in the three institutional types.

Sango-Jordan's study used data from the 1986 HS&B follow-up to explore four economic/employment outcomes: full-time employment, average 1985 annual income, formal training for the job currently held, and job skills learned in school. It found no statistical significance in the full-time employment of those who worked by educational sector. Full-time employ-

. . . public vocational students were significantly more satisfied with their training than the students who had attended private career schools.

9. This section on NAVE measures of economic and employment outcomes is derived from Goodwin 1989, pp. 64–69.

ment by sector between March 1984 and February 1986 was 88 percent for private career school attendees, 85 percent for four-year college attendees, and 83 percent for community college, public technical institute, and other less than four-year attendees (Sango-Jordan 1989).

Data on workers' average income for 1985 are more compelling. As table 8 shows, for those who held full-time jobs during 1984 to 1986, proprietary school students earned somewhat more than those in other sectors. For those who obtained a license, certificate, or degree, this difference between the private career school and other sectors was even more pronounced. Equally interesting is the fact that those who attended a proprietary school but did not receive a postsecondary credential earned less than students from other sectors.[10]

TABLE 8

AVERAGE INCOME IN 1985 FOR INDIVIDUALS WITH AND WITHOUT POSTSECONDARY CREDENTIALS AS OF FEBRUARY 1986: From the HS&B Survey

Educational Option	No Postsecondary Credential	License, Degree, or Certificate	Total
Not enrolled	$12,770	$12,705	$12,758
Private career	$12,217	$14,061	$13,224
Other less than four-year	$12,884	$12,739	$12,819
Four-year plus	$12,468	$12,943	$12,736
Total	$12,710	$12,914	$12,789

Source: Sango-Jordan 1989, p. 32.

The study further found that 50 percent of the private career school graduates reported they had been formally trained for the jobs they currently held. Approximately 47 percent of the students who had attended four-year colleges and 41 percent of those who were enrolled in other less than four-year programs reported receiving formal training for their current jobs. Similarly, 40 percent of the proprietary school graduates indicated they had learned most of their current job skills in school, compared to 34 percent of those who had enrolled in other schools.

---

10. For an interesting early study of the effects on lifetime income of graduating from a private career school, see Freeman 1974.

Comparisons among the sectors in terms of outcomes is, in part, misleading. Each sector has distinct missions and goals and enrolls students for varying lengths of time. Community colleges contend that many of their students are not seeking a degree or certificate but are interested in developing competency in a special area that may require only a few classes and not a degree. And HS&B data do not include those who may be taking longer than six years to complete a degree.

POLICY ISSUES

Private career schools became a front-burner issue for post-secondary education policy about the mid-1980s. Though concern about the schools had been raised previously, in terms of participation in federal programs and in broader discussions about consumer rights and abuses, the level of interest raised during that time was unprecedented. The impetus for this increased interest can be traced to one key indicator: rapid increases in the amounts defaulted by students participating in federally guaranteed student loan programs. As research examining the reasons for the increased defaults began to be released, the findings were surprising to many—students in proprietary schools were found to default at twice the rate as students in other sectors, causing a firestorm of criticism and scrutiny of private career schools that continues to the present.

The sudden interest in proprietary schools generated by the debate over default led to several subsequent policy discussions. One had to do with the level of debt appropriate for young people entering the labor market, another with the increasing proportion of overall federal funds for student assistance going to students in private career schools, and another with consumer rights and abuses related to admissions, advertising, and promises for employment.

Still another reawakened interest was state licensing because of the states' historical role in having primary responsibility for the oversight and regulation of education. Accrediting also spurred new interest in the issue of its requirement for institutional eligibility for federal student aid funds. Clearly, these policy areas are interrelated. The debates reflect a broad interest in the general operation of proprietary schools and the quality of education they provide.

Governmental Assistance for Students and Schools

As noted earlier, student aid has been an important part of the financing equation for students in all sectors of post-secondary education since the passage of the 1972 Education Amendments. Since that time, federal student aid for proprietary school students has greatly increased, and the relative share of student aid awarded to students in other sectors has declined as a result. The increasing number of private career school students in the program has reduced funds for students in other sectors, an important factor in the strained relationship between the private career school sector and traditional higher education in Washington, D.C.

This subsection is concerned with the literature's discussion of four areas related to this support: (1) which students and how many receive student assistance and at what level of support; (2) other public support for private career school students and schools; (3) rates of student loan default and the correlates of loan default; and (4) consumer rights and abuses.

Student aid

Proprietary school students receive assistance from a variety of sources, including federal, state, institutional, and private sources, but the vast majority of their support comes from the federal government. Federal student aid programs provide about 80 percent of the total financial aid received by proprietary school students. They include the Pell Grant program, the Stafford Student Loan program (which includes three components: Stafford loans, Parent Loans for Undergraduate Students, and Supplemental Loans for Students), the Supplemental Educational Opportunity Grant (SEOG) program, the State Student Incentive Grant (SSIG) program, the College Work Study (CWS) program, and the Perkins Loan (formerly National Direct Student Loan) program.

According to the 1987 NPSAS, about 81 percent of private career school students receive some form of student assistance, compared to approximately 69 percent of students in private colleges, 40 percent of students in public institutions, and about 46 percent of all postsecondary students. In terms of the federal student aid programs, nearly 76 percent of proprietary school students receive federal assistance based on need, compared to 49 percent of private college students, 26 percent of students at public institutions, and 33 percent of all postsecondary students (Choy and Gifford 1990, p. 75).

The NPSAS also found that about 53 percent of proprietary school students received a grant in 1986 and about 70 percent received a loan. In contrast, 35 percent of all students received a grant and 25 percent received a loan. Clearly, these data suggest that private career school students rely heavily on student aid in general and on federal assistance in particular.

One interesting phenomenon that has occurred virtually unabated since 1972 is a gradual increase in the percentage of total federal aid going to proprietary school students. Many in traditional higher education view this occurrence with alarm, as nonentitlement dollars must increasingly be shared with private career school students.

As table 9 shows, proprietary schools' share of the campus-based programs (SEOG, CWS, and Perkins) since 1980 has remained fairly level, rising slightly in the last two years. Private career schools' share of Pell grants more than doubled during this period, however. Students in proprietary schools received more than one-quarter of the $4.5 billion in Pell grants, or $1.1 billion of the funds available in 1988–89 (College Board 1990).

TABLE 9

PERCENTAGE DISTRIBUTION OF AID FROM THE PELL AND CAMPUS-BASED PROGRAMS, BY CONTROL OF INSTITUTION: 1980-81 to 1988-89

	80-81	81-82	82-83	83-84	84-85	85-86	86-87	87-88	Estimated 88-89
Pell Grants									
Public	59.7	59.5	56.9	56.5	56.2	55.8	54.4	53.3	55.3
Private	28.8	27.1	26.6	24.6	23.0	21.9	20.7	20.1	20.2
Private career	11.5	13.5	16.6	18.8	20.8	22.1	24.9	26.6	24.5
Campus-based Programs									
Public	53.0	52.9	53.2	52.4	52.4	51.4	51.5	50.8	51.1
Private	41.8	42.0	42.0	42.5	42.7	43.3	42.9	43.4	43.8
Private career	5.2	5.1	4.9	5.1	4.9	5.3	5.6	5.8	5.2

Source: College Board 1990.

Data on the share of Stafford loans going to private career school students are more limited and therefore less reliable. Most reliable estimates, however, suggest that at least 35 percent of all Stafford loans go to proprietary school borrowers (see, e.g., Hauptman and Merisotis 1989). A much larger percentage of the Supplemental Loans for Students program awards went to private career school students in 1987–88 (U.S. General Accounting Office 1989), although policy changes since that time will probably reverse that trend. Based on these figures, the total dollar amount in loans going to proprietary school students during academic year 1987–88 was more than $4 billion.

Information on the annual dollar amount of student aid received by private career school students is extremely hard to locate because of the lack of a consistent annual student aid survey. The NPSAS found that proprietary school students actually receive less aid per student from *all* sources than students at private colleges and that aid per student for recipients from all sources amounted to $5,633 a year for private college students, $2,887 for public college students, $4,025 for proprietary school students, and $3,813 for all postsecondary students. Traditional college students are more likely to receive assistance from state, private, and institutional sources than private career school students, but private career school students received more federal aid than students in other sectors. According to the NPSAS, proprietary school students (who received aid) received $3,630 in federal aid per student in 1986–87, compared to $3,525 for private college students, $2,616 for students attending public institutions, and $2,973 for all postsecondary students who received aid (Korb et al. 1988, p. 37).

Data on student aid for proprietary school students from nonfederal sources are limited. The only relevant state information is eligibility of proprietary school students for state student aid awards. According to a survey of state agencies that provide grants to postsecondary students, more than two-thirds of all states provide some state grant support to students attending private career schools, although most states exclude private career school students from unlimited participation. Students at these schools received close to $100 million in state grant aid, or less than 10 percent of all state grants awarded, in 1988–89 (Reeher and Davis 1989).

In general, proprietary school students depend heavily on federal student aid, especially Pell grants and Stafford loans. According to one researcher, "Administrators tend to depend on federal financial aid programs" as they use them more (Schaeffer 1979, p. 26). This high level of use of student aid will be of continuing concern to policy makers interested in the allocation of federal student aid dollars.

Other programs of student support

Discussion of private career schools in the current policy environment is almost exclusively about federal student aid programs. For reasons cited earlier, the reliance of proprietary school students and schools on federal aid necessarily has dictated much of this scrutiny. Nevertheless, students and schools receive support in other ways. While the information available about private career school students' use of these other programs is minimal, it is important to at least mention them to help provide a better picture of proprietary schools.

The largest source of nonstudent aid for private career school students is training for veterans, available chiefly through the new GI Bill. Schools become eligible for the GI Bill by approval of a state agency. Accreditation is not required as it is for the federal Title IV student aid programs. Program rules generally require vocational schools receiving aid to meet certain performance-based standards, such as placing at least 50 percent of all students in jobs for which they were trained.

Data on participation in veterans' programs by proprietary school students are not available for recent years. The number of veterans in private career schools dropped sharply in the 1970s, however, from 810,000 in 1974 to 190,000 in 1980 (Wilms 1982, pp. 4, 5) because of reductions in funding for veterans' programs.

Proprietary schools can also receive federal government funds through the Job Training Partnership Act (JTPA) to train students in specific job areas. Unfortunately, no national data are available on participation in JTPA training by private career school students. According to unpublished data from a survey of NATTS-accredited schools in 1988, however, less than 2 percent of all students enrolled in NATTS schools were trained through the auspices of JTPA. Total revenues from JTPA for NATTS schools were also relatively insignificant—less than $20 million nationally.

Vocational rehabilitation funds might also be used to fund training for students at proprietary schools. According to the NATTS survey, approximately 10 percent of all NATTS students receive some funds through vocational rehabilitation, though again the total dollar amount—perhaps $25 million—is nearly negligible.

Student loan defaults
The bulk of the discussion generated since the mid-1980s about private career schools has centered on the fact that students attending proprietary schools default on their guaranteed student loans at a much higher rate than students in other types of institutions.[11] This "revelation" has caused probably the greatest activity at both the federal and state lev-

11. Some of the discussion in this subsection is derived from Merisotis 1989.

els that has been seen in the student aid arena since the inception of the major federal programs.

The reasons for this intense interest are multidimensional. One is purely budgetary: Defaults cost the federal government money because of the federal guarantee that repays lenders for every defaulted loan. As borrowing under the Stafford program soared in the late 1970s and early 1980s, the dollar volume in defaults also increased. Eventually, about 1986, concern about the amount of loans being defaulted fueled the intense policy debate about defaults that has continued nearly unabated into the 1990s.

Other financial concerns are important in the policy debate. For example, each loan is actually guaranteed by a state-level (or in some cases national) guarantee agency that is reimbursed by the federal government for defaults paid to banks and other lenders originating the loans. Guarantee agencies participate in a risk-sharing arrangement with the federal government by agreeing to keep defaults below a certain level. If defaults exceed these minimum levels, the guarantee agency is reimbursed less than 100 percent on the loans. Guarantee agencies therefore have an important interest in keeping defaults below this federal trigger to avoid losing revenue.

The lending institutions themselves, though they assume no risk in making the loan, have a stake in defaults because of the administrative burden incurred by a delinquent (and subsequently defaulted) borrower. Federal "due diligence" regulations require the lender to follow precise procedures for contacting delinquent students and informing them of their status. Failure to do so is grounds for the federal government to restrict the lending claim.[12] Lenders resist making loans to high-risk students because of the increased costs of administration and the risk the claim might be rejected.

Concerns about the effects of defaulting on students, particularly those from low-income backgrounds, have also played a part in this debate. The long-term consequences of defaulting—ruined credit, onerous collection fees, and the denial of further postsecondary educational opportunity (because defaulters cannot receive other federal student

---

12. For a blow-by-blow account of one such incident that involved close to a half billion dollars in loans, see Scholl 1989.

aid)—are significant, and the impact on individuals is not fully understood.

The purpose here is not to recount the entire student loan default picture to the present, a somewhat futile exercise. The debate over defaults that hit its stride in the mid-1980s helped to produce voluminous research on who defaults, but it has unfortunately been only marginally helpful in describing *why* students default.

Since 1980, several reports and studies have been generated to investigate the problem of student loan defaults. They generally fall into two groups: those that report or analyze default statistics of a general nature (reports on the dollar amounts and number of defaults in a group of states or nationally or papers that analyze the ways in which program default rates are reported or analyzed, for example) and those that identify correlates of defaults (by educational sector, characteristics of individual borrowers, and so on) and often suggest remedies.

One effort to obtain a national portrait of student loan defaults was undertaken by a group called Federal Funds Information for States (associated with the National Guarantors Association and the National Council of State Legislators), which tracks federal programs designed to assist states. The resulting study (Wolfe, Osman, and Miller 1987) for the first time compiled national statistics on the dollar amounts and rates of default by institution and included information summarizing state default rates. The data were obtained from U.S. Department of Education computer records of nearly 13 million student loans insured by guarantee agencies through the Guaranteed Student Loan (GSL) program, the so-called "state tape dump."

The report revealed some of the most comprehensive information on defaults at the institutional level ever collected up to that point. For example, 427 institutions were identified as having default rates greater than 60 percent, accounting for almost 5 percent of all participating institutions. Approximately 60 percent of the institutions had default rates less than 20 percent. Furthermore, the report notes that, of the $36.3 billion cumulative loans in repayment (excluding federally insured student loans), $4.4 billion, or approximately 12.1 percent, had been defaulted through 1986. The study was widely criticized at the time because the data base included many errors. One problem was that the list included

. . . higher levels of indebtedness improve the likelihood of repayment, and knowledge of when repayment begins is nearly twice as high for repayers than for defaulters.

institutions that were no longer in business, thus tending to overstate the overall problem with defaults on a state-by-state or national basis (see, e.g., National Association 1987).

A more recent study shows annual and cumulative default rates from 1975 through 1986 (Lee 1988b). Notably, the data (shown in table 10) show little variance in the rates since the middle 1970s. The furor over defaults that occurred in the middle 1980s appears to have been the result of total dollars defaulted (reflecting increased borrowing) rather than a stark increase in the incidence of default.

TABLE 10

COMPARISON OF ANNUAL AND CUMULATIVE RATES OF DEFAULT: 1975 to 1986

Year	Repayment ($000,000)	Default ($000,000)	Annual Rate (percent)	Cumulative Rate (percent)
1975	2,560	129	5.0	8.2
1976	2,651	194	7.3	9.9
1977	2,783	202	7.3	10.9
1978	2,925	208	7.1	11.6
1979	3,200	223	7.0	12.0
1980	3,762	239	6.4	12.5
1981	4,711	254	5.4	12.3
1982	6,856	288	4.2	11.2
1983	9,525	531	5.6	10.8
1984	12,959	713	5.5	10.9
1985	16,473	1,032	6.3	11.6
1986	20,591	1,371	6.7	12.6

Source: Lee 1988b.

A much larger body of literature concerns where or how high rates of default are concentrated. The characteristics of borrowers who default and the types of institutions they attend are the most common areas of analysis.

Studies concerned primarily with the individual character-istics of borrowers who default on their loans are the most common (see, e.g., Lee 1982). Among the findings are that borrowers in their first few years of repayment are more likely to default than those who have maintained good standing for two years and that students in two-year public institutions and private career schools have higher rates of default than those in four-year programs. As of 1981, an estimated 12.16 percent of all loans guaranteed by guarantee agencies (and having entered repayment) ended in default (Lee 1982).

Another study, by the New York guarantee agency, examined the characteristics of borrowers who default through an analysis of those who graduated or left school in 1982 and were scheduled to begin repayment in 1983 (New York State Higher Education 1984). It found that employment and default are inversely related, the number of years spent in school and default are inversely related, higher levels of indebtedness improve the likelihood of repayment, and knowledge of when repayment begins is nearly twice as high for repayers than for defaulters.

The negative correlation of a borrower's income to default is one relationship that has surfaced continually in the research. A study of 4,000 defaulters from Virginia, for example, found that 77 percent of defaulters came from families whose incomes were less than $20,000 at the time of the loan's origination (Ehlenfeldt and Springfield 1984). In contrast, borrowers whose family incomes were over $40,000 accounted for less than 3 percent of total defaults. A later study, this one of borrowers at community colleges and proprietary schools in California, also found that family income is significantly related to defaulting (Wilms, Moore, and Bolus 1987).

The other important factor related to defaulting is dropping out of the school program. One study from the middle 1980s, for example, notes that over 50 percent of Pennsylvania defaulters were first-year students who dropped out of school but had probably taken out only one loan. Such students make up a significant portion of the defaulting population (Davis 1985). Other, later studies confirm this finding, with some suggesting that dropping out may be attributed to poor academic preparation, low motivation, or dissatisfaction with a postsecondary program, which in turn may lead to default (Wilms, Moore, and Bolus 1987).

All of these factors lead to the more central question of the incidence of default by sector. Studies that examine the effect of institutional type on default have sometimes been viewed as controversial, because, given the structure of the student loan system, institutions themselves have no direct control over the borrower to influence his or her repayment. Nevertheless, the studies are an important part of the policy debate

and essential to understanding private career schools and what they do.

Most of the studies using data on type and control of institution have found that proprietary and other vocational schools and, usually to a lesser extent, community colleges, have the highest rates of default. One study, for example, notes that borrowers who last attended vocational schools were twice as likely to default as borrowers from two-year institutions (17.2 percent versus 8.6 percent) (New York State Higher Education 1984). Borrowers from four-year institutions defaulted less than 5 percent of the time. The report attributes the differences to earlier findings that default and the number of years in school are inversely related.

A study of GSL borrowers in California from 1985 found the rates of default for private career schools and two-year institutions to be similar (California Postsecondary Education Commission 1985). The study found the lowest rate of default for public four-year schools (4.6 percent), with proprietary schools (21.7 percent) and community colleges (17.8 percent) showing much higher rates.

A comparison of default rates by sector using data from five states found private career and two-year institutions to be disproportionately represented in their share of defaults (Merisotis 1988). As table 11 shows, in four of the five states, proprietary schools had default shares more than twice or nearly twice the level of their share of loan volume. The study also suggests that differences between states bear an important relationship to the likelihood of default, warning that any sort of national policy geared toward any one educational sector would likely have limited success. Data from two of the states show that students from different cohorts and varying income levels showed a considerable variance in their propensity for defaulting, supporting the idea that sectoral differences in default rates may at least be partially explained by differences in borrowers' characteristics.

More recent research on the determinants of default have addressed the question of whether the characteristics of borrowers can be used to explain the higher rates of default noted at private career schools. In a study of borrowers in California, a state that has weathered significant losses resulting from defaults on GSLs, the disadvantaged socioeconomic status of students attending proprietary and two-year schools was found to be most strongly correlated with the likelihood

TABLE 11

CUMULATIVE PERCENT DISTRIBUTION OF LOAN VOLUME AND DOLLARS DEFAULTED IN FIVE STATES, BY SECTOR: Through FY 1987

	Proprietary	Two-year Public	Four-year Public	Four-year Private	Two-year Private	Other
California						
Loan percent	18.0	11.6	32.8	28.6	2.0	7.0
Default percent	34.3	21.6	20.4	17.6	2.1	4.0
Illinois						
Loan percent	10.4	8.6	40.6	27.5	1.9	11.0
Default percent	24.0	15.0	31.4	21.1	2.9	5.6
Massachusetts						
Loan percent	5.2	3.3	24.5	58.0	2.5	6.5
Default percent	12.7	7.0	23.6	45.5	5.2	6.0
New Jersey						
Loan percent	30.8	10.9	31.2	21.4	NA	5.7
Default percent	37.8	13.3	28.4	15.4	NA	5.1
Pennsylvania						
Loan percent	16.5	3.4	39.2	38.1	1.1	1.7
Default percent	35.0	5.9	30.9	26.1	1.2	0.9

NA = Not available.

Source: Merisotis 1988, p. 22.

of default, and institutional practices were found to be of limited importance (Wilms, Moore, and Bolus 1986). Another study, postulating that economic variables it did not measure were most likely responsible for racial differences, looked exclusively at students in California's private career schools and community colleges and found that a student's background characteristics, most notably race, are strongly associated with defaulting (Wilms, Moore, and Bolus 1987).

One of the most recent large-scale state studies on GSLs (California Student Aid Commission 1988) confirms many of the earlier findings. Using cumulative data on defaulters participating in California's GSL program, the study found that defaulters:

• Are likely to have attended community colleges and proprietary schools;
• Have, regardless of institutional sector, significantly lower family incomes at the time the loan is made;

- Are often borrowers who only borrow in their first year or who have taken out only one loan; and
- Usually do *not* enter default because of high loan balances or an excessive "debt burden," as conventional wisdom might suggest.

The data from this study suggest that future efforts to investigate student loan defaults need to focus on factors that take borrowers' characteristics and, perhaps even more important, their attitudes into fuller account.

A default risk index using the NPSAS data on out-of-school borrowers rates students according to characteristics associated with the ability to succeed in the labor market and the resources they might have available to deal with financial problems (Lee 1990c). The index was developed as follows:

White/Asian = 0	African-American/Hispanic = 1
Male = 0	Female = 1
Single or married = 0	Divorced or widowed = 2
No dependents = 0	Dependents = 1
High socioeconomic background = 0	Low socioeconomic background = 1

A white, single male with no dependents from a high socioeconomic background has a risk score of zero. An African-American divorced mother from a low socioeconomic background has a risk score of six. The risk score is related both to the probability of defaulting and to the probability of having been enrolled in a private career school (see table 12).

Relationships exist between the risk score and the chances of defaulting and between the risk score and enrollment in a non-degree-granting school. High-risk students are more likely to enroll in short, specific vocational programs. The results of the regression model are consistent with the earlier study (California Student Aid Commission 1988), suggesting that students' characteristics are more important than type of institution for understanding default.

Using records from nine of the largest guarantee agencies in the country, a study of default rates in the Supplemental Loans for Students program, which experienced a tremendous increase in loan volume in the three years from 1986 to 1989 as a result of the 1986 Higher Education Amendments, found that annual levels of default on these loans increased from

TABLE 12

PERSONAL RISK SCORE AND DEFAULT RATES

Risk Score	Percent Defaulting	Percent Enrolling in Non-Degree-Granting School
0	10.0	12.4
1	13.8	22.4
2	14.3	26.9
3	19.0	31.0
4	27.8	40.0
5	50.2	56.1
6	56.8	64.5
Average	**22.1**	**32.8**

Source: Lee 1990c, p. 31.

$14 million in 1987 to $50 million in 1988 to $247 million in 1989 (U.S. General Accounting Office 1989). Defaults by proprietary school borrowers increased from 12 percent of defaults on Supplemental Loans for Students in 1987 to 86 percent in 1989. The study was an important tool used by congressional reformers to limit access to Supplemental Loans for private career school students in P.L. 101–239 (which actually limits access for students attending schools with high default rates).

The U.S. Department of Education took steps in 1989 to limit defaults on student loans, especially in proprietary schools. Though the regulations do not mention private career schools, it is clear from the debates leading up to the issuance of these regulations that they are primarily the target of the rules (see 34 CFR 668). The new requirements, among other things, mandate that institutions with a default rate for a fiscal year above 60 percent are to be limited, suspended, or terminated from the Stafford program; that those with default rates between 40 to 60 percent are required to lower such rates by 5 percent a year to continue participating in federal loan programs; that those with default rates of 20 to 60 percent must adopt Department-approved "default management plans"; that all schools must provide entrance counseling to first-time borrowers; and that schools providing vocational training must disclose certain information to prospective students, including job placement and program completion rates. This instance is the first in which some form of measuring outcomes is tied to institutional participation in federal student aid programs.

In the waning days of the 101st Congress, other restraints on schools with high default rates were also imposed. Schools with default rates (as defined in the law) above 35 percent were targeted for program suspension, beginning in fiscal year 1992, although historically black and tribal colleges were given extensions to achieve the goals (Bauman 1990).

Consumer rights and abuses

The rights of private career school students as consumers and the alleged abuse of those rights by school operators are important, recurring topics in the literature. As noted earlier, concerns about students' being taken advantage of by unscrupulous schools can be traced back to the earlier part of the 20th century. Since then, the issue has been discussed extensively, and legislation and regulations have been implemented at the federal, state, and local levels. To at least some extent, these efforts have been less successful than hoped, largely because of an almost total void in understanding about the pervasiveness or character of the problem, which limits discussion about the need for and methods of improving consumer rights. In addition, state and federal agencies' commitment to oversight has been spotty.

Consumer rights is a topic with broad implications. It refers not only to unfair practices in terms of recruiting students and charging them tuition, but also to who has what responsibility for protecting those rights. This subsection is limited to the former, concentrating on the nuts and bolts of consumer rights from students' perspective. The rights of students compared to their financial investment in postsecondary education is of special interest here; the next subsection, on licensing and accreditation, examines the mechanics of consumer rights and changes recommended.

Three "waves" of interest have occurred in the consumer rights of proprietary school students. The first occurred after World War II and related to the GI program. The second occurred in the early and middle 1970s and coincided with the broader consumer movement that swept the country at the time. And the third wave began in the mid-1980s and has continued into the 1990s.

According to contemporary accounts, the Federal Trade Commission (FTC) took a compelling interest in the private career school sector in response to journalistic and other public exposures of deceptive sales and recruiting practices in the late 1960s.[13] The FTC's exploration was exhaustive; hearings on the issue were held for over six years, from 1970 through 1976, and testimony—both pro and con—was compiled from over 900 witnesses as to deceptive and fraudulent recruitment practices (Wilms 1982, p. 4).

Based on the findings, the FTC concluded that several factors were to blame for these apparent abuses of consumer rights. One was a lack of reliable information available to students that allowed them to verify claims made by schools. Another was the availability of federal student aid, which the Commission said seemed like "free money" to students and therefore led them to make poor enrollment decisions. Further, these abuses were partly motivated by the fact that student aid provided schools with incentives to enroll students regardless of their ability to benefit from the training (Federal Trade Commission 1976).

In 1978, the FTC issued a proposed trade regulation rule that would have required schools to provide students with information about graduation rates, establish policies for pro-rated refunds of tuition, and implement a process by which an enrollment agreement would automatically be canceled unless it were reaffirmed. The proprietary school sector successfully challenged the rule in late 1979, however (Wilms 1982, p. 5). Representatives of the sector argued that the rule would punish all schools for the transgressions of a few. After several attempts to revise the rule, all unsuccessful, the FTC appears to have let the issue die quietly without achieving its objective of national accountability standards for private career schools.

In addition to the information gathered for and disseminated by the FTC, the literature is rich with other anecdotal information on the abuse of consumer rights by proprietary schools. The literature generally concurs that "abuse" occurs when some condition is created that causes the student to make a decision based on inaccurate or deceptive information

---

13. For an excellent review of the events in this debate through 1975, see Jung et al. 1976, pp. 9–28.

or make a decision not in his or her best interest. These abuses can take many shapes (see table 13), although little information is available on the frequency of problems in these areas.

The studies that examine consumer abuse (or complaints of abuse) generally attempt to catalog those abuses and then offer remedies. A study from the mid-1970s, for example, collected information on consumer rights from both institutions and enrolled students (Jung et al. 1976) but did not attempt to systematically collect information on the extent or magnitude of consumer abuses. Instead, it concentrated on the potential for abuse, based on variables designed to measure ways in which schools might violate students' rights. The researchers found that some abuses occur at all levels of postsecondary education and suggested that remedies designed to protect consumer rights should apply to all institutions.

Consumer rights could be more adequately protected by the federal government in several ways. Most crucial are disseminating information to institutions on the categories, examples, and indicators of potentially abusive practices; publishing and disseminating information on consumer rights

TABLE 13

POSSIBLE CONSUMER ABUSES

- Inequitable refund policies and failure to refund tuition and fees in a timely manner.
- Misleading recruitment and admissions practices.
- Untrue or misleading advertising.
- Inadequate instructional programs.
- Unqualified instructional staff.
- Lack of necessary disclosure in written documents.
- Inadequate instructional equipment and facilities.
- Lack of adequate job placement services and lack of adequate follow-through.
- Lack of adequate student selection and orientation practices.
- Inadequate housing.
- Lack of adequate record keeping.
- Excessive instability in the instructional staff.
- Misrepresentation or misuse of chartered, approved, or accredited status.
- Lack of adequate financial stability.

Source: Jung et al. 1976, p. 3.

directed at students nationwide; considering the establishment of minimum federal consumer protection standards; and providing states with technical and financial support to develop or augment institutional monitoring systems to prevent abuse.

A decade after this study was conducted, the same office in the Department of Education initiated another one (Fitzgerald and Harmon 1988). It coincided with the most recent wave of interest in consumer rights for postsecondary students, and this period of concern will probably culminate with the 1991 reauthorization of the Higher Education Act.

Like the earlier study, this one did not attempt to estimate the frequency, severity, or magnitude of problems with violations of consumer rights. The project's staff relied primarily on interviews with federal government officials, state and guarantee agency representatives, and institutional administrators. Unlike the first study, it focused on proprietary schools almost exclusively. The study was criticized for its methodological flaws, primarily because "the evidence collected does not appear to have shaped the major conclusions or interpretations made by the authors of the paper" (Yin 1988, p. 1). Nevertheless, the study does highlight areas of concern for those interested in consumer rights.

For example, while provisions for accreditation are adequate to protect basic consumer rights, competition (schools simply jumping from one accrediting body to another) and lengthy due process procedures hamper effective regulation by accrediting organizations. Recruiting materials used by some schools are deceptive or incomplete. And some schools abuse the "ability-to-benefit" provisions in federal statutes designed to allow the admission of students who have not received a high school degree or equivalent if the student can demonstrate an ability to benefit from the postsecondary training. Recent changes in federal regulations and accreditation standards have addressed problems of tuition refunds, misstatement of completion and placement rates, changes in accreditation, and inadequate staffing, but the effects of these changes are not currently known.

Nearly all [ability-to-benefit] students surveyed indicated satisfaction with their courses, teachers, and facilities.

One of the only known comprehensive studies of the use of ability-to-benefit provisions by private career schools suggests that common wisdom about their incidence of use may be exaggerated (see Sango-Jordan 1988). Using a weighted sample of students in the 1987 NPSAS, the study found that approximately 270,000 students were classified as "ability-to-benefit students" in 1987. Of that number, an estimated 144,000, or just over half of the total group, attended proprietary schools. Many of the community college ability-to-benefit students attended part time and did not receive student aid. Overall, about 9 percent of all private career school students were admitted to programs based on ability to benefit in 1987.

Regrettably, the survey sample used to extrapolate these data was small, and, as a result, the number of ability-to-benefit students in the sample was also limited. This factor could subject the study to some criticism for methodological weakness; nevertheless, it does suggest that the misuse of ability-to-benefit provisions by proprietary schools as an example of abusive practices may be overstated.

A forthcoming study of NATTS students found that ability-to-benefit students enrolled in these schools primarily because of program offerings and the school's reputation were also very pleased with their choice (Career Training Foundation 1991). Nearly all students surveyed indicated satisfaction with their courses, teachers, and facilities.

Because so little is known about consumer rights in postsecondary education, much more research needs to be conducted to determine the causes of abuse, its overall incidence, and ways in which it might be prevented. A study by the U.S. Department of Education's Office of Policy, Budget, and Evaluation will examine the extent to which information about consumer rights is and can be made available and test and evaluate mechanisms for providing this information (U.S. Dept. of Education 1991). Such research is of considerable value in the policy arena, given misgivings and concerns about the effect of consumer protection relative to federal programs.

Licensing and Accreditation
How private career schools are regulated largely depends on state licensing and accreditation. Both of these functions play an important role in determining eligibility for federal student aid programs. Both have been scrutinized by researchers when concerns regarding proprietary schools' participation in student aid programs have surfaced. And both will likely continue to be studied into the 1990s as pressure to change the student aid programs builds because of budgetary, economic, and demographic concerns.

State licensing and accreditation are part of a tripartite system of determining eligibility for federal student assistance programs. The three legs of this system require an institution applying for eligibility to:

1. Be legally authorized to operate in the state where it is located;
2. Be accredited by a private, nongovernmental accrediting body officially recognized by the U.S. Department of Education; and
3. Meet the specific provisions of student aid programs, whether general requirements or program-specific criteria.

This subsection is concerned primarily with the first two legs of the triad, specifically the role of state licensing in ensuring the quality of proprietary school education and the nature of accreditation.

State licensing

Since 1985, all 50 states and the District of Columbia have laws establishing requirements for licensure of private career schools. Each state has some agency responsible for planning and policy development for proprietary schools, though structural organization varies considerably across states.

Most states assign oversight of private career schools to different agencies—one for degree-granting and one for non-degree-granting institutions. Degree-granting schools are often, but not always, regulated by the same agency that regulates higher education institutions—a state board (or department) of higher education in many states. Non-degree-granting schools, which make up the bulk of proprietary schools, are usually regulated by other state agencies. States often are responsible for licensing unaccredited as well as accredited schools.

It is useful to think about state licensing of private career schools by considering the broad organizational types with authority to regulate these schools: a department of higher education, a department of education, a separate state agency, and an independent proprietary commission.[14]

---

14. The first three types are historical categories, but the independent commission appears to be a more recent phenomenon. For a discussion of the historical categories, see Bender 1976.

According to a survey conducted in the mid-1970s, about two-thirds of all states had vested licensing authority for most non-degree-granting institutions in a department of education. The remainder were split between the department of higher education, which also regulated the degree-granting institutions in most states, and separate agencies (Bender 1976). Though no recent comprehensive surveys of state practices have been conducted, this arrangement would appear to conform generally to modern structures (Mingle 1989).

The oversight of proprietary schools is complicated in many states by the fact that multiple state agencies have varying responsibilities for different types of private career schools and programs. Not only is oversight for degree-granting institutions separated from that for non-degree-granting institutions; many states also treat various occupational categories separately from the general approval system. For example, many states license schools of cosmetology through state licensing boards that also license practitioners (cosmetologists and hairstylists) and salons. In some states, this system is quite cumbersome. A study of proprietary schools in New Jersey, for example, found that licensing authority is vested not only in the state Department of Education and Higher Education and the Board of Cosmetology, but also in the state Department of Labor (which regulates schools with service provider contracts under JTPA), the Division of Motor Vehicles (which regulates schools for drivers of tractor trailers), the Casino Control Commission (which regulates schools for casino dealers), the Department of Health (which regulates nursing schools and programs), and other agencies (New Jersey Interagency Task Force 1990). California instituted a new structure in 1989 that attempts to avoid this confusion by consolidating all authority in one separate agency specifically designed to regulate private career schools, a model that was previously used in Indiana and a handful of other states.

State licensing serves three basic functions. First, it protects students from unscrupulous schools by requiring minimum educational standards to which all schools must adhere. Second, it protects the state's financial stake in the students and schools—through student aid, state vocational training programs, or other means—by requiring schools to meet certain financial criteria. Third, it protects schools (and students) from unfair competition by other schools through limits on misleading advertising, unethical recruiting, and other illegal competitive practices. Each function is incorporated into the same laws and regulations governing proprietary schools.

A study of state oversight of private career schools in the mid-1980s offered 10 categories of criteria for licensing in state regulations: purposes and objectives, administration and governance, finances, curriculum and program of studies, faculty, physical plant, library, student services, admissions, and refund policy, publications, and college records (Chaloux 1985). Unfortunately, it is impossible to summarize specific state licensing requirements because of the tremendous variation within and among states. It could be instructive, however, to examine the following list of licensing requirements for one state, Ohio. Each school is required to:

1. File a completed application with the owner's signature notarized;
2. Provide a check payable to the Treasurer, State of Ohio, for $375.00;
3. Provide a $10,000 surety bond;
4. Provide a $1,000 blanket bond for each agent;
5. Provide a school catalog;
6. Provide an enrollment agreement;
7. Provide a refund policy;
8. List qualifications for teachers and directors;
9. Provide a "facilities compliance statement";
10. Provide evidence that requirements for the curriculum are being met; and
11. Provide proof of financial responsibility (Jones 1987).

Most of the discussion about state regulation of private career schools concentrates on what is wrong with state licensing and suggests remedies for these problems. Several reports produced in the late 1980s, for example, describe these problems and the proposed solutions.

The most consistent problem with state regulation of proprietary schools appears to be inadequate financial standards, especially those that protect students in the event of the school's sudden closure and insolvency. Schools that suddenly close often fail to reimburse students for lost tuition and incomplete services, and surety bonds are frequently inadequate to repay all students. Several recent state reports note this problem (California Postsecondary Education Commission 1989a; New Jersey Interagency Task Force 1990; Tennessee Higher Education Commission 1989). The proposed solution, offered by legislators and regulators in several states, is the establishment of a tuition recovery fund. The Student Tuition Recovery Fund in California, for example, reimburses a student for prepaid tuition should the school suddenly close. Institutions are required to collect assessments per student (or pay on behalf of students) and remit them to the fund. If a school closes and the state is unable to collect from the school's owners (or the bonding is inadequate), students can be repaid through the fund. States also have developed "train-out" or "teach-out" provisions to provide similar training to students at a different school.

State licensing has also been rendered partially ineffective because of limited legal powers. New York, for example, found that its state licensing system was hampered by legal obstacles that made the enforcement of existing laws nearly impossible. The state Education Department recommended that several of these powers be strengthened:

1. The ability to deny a license to a school if the owner has been convicted of a felony or is subject to criminal penalties in other states;
2. The ability to deny a license if stockholders in a school once owned another school that has outstanding claims against it;
3. The ability to require certified financial statements;
4. The ability to review annually qualifications for licensure;
5. The ability to develop a train-out program (New York State Education 1989).

Another issue related to state licensing that has been discussed less in the literature is the fact that many states exempt accredited schools from a full licensure review.[15] In effect, these states assume that accreditation standards ensure educational quality—a contention that has been contested for several years. The problem arises because "accrediting agencies often use the obtaining of a state license as the first step

---

15. Exemption for accredited institutions was part of the model legislation proposed by the Education Commission of the States in 1973. This model legislation had a significant effect on licensing laws subsequently adopted in many states. See Education Commission of the States 1973.

toward full accreditation status" (Mingle 1989, p. 4), which has led to a chicken-versus-egg phenomenon—which comes first, the license or the accreditation?—that has yet to be resolved.

A segment of the literature on private career schools, contributed to by both supporters and detractors of the schools, argues that a central problem with state regulation of proprietary schools is poor enforcement of existing laws. For example, the majority of problems with the oversight and regulation of private career schools result from poor enforcement rather than major problems with existing laws (Stewart and Spille 1988). Another report, while supporting calls for overhauling existing laws and rules, also notes that poor enforcement is a significant problem and argues that regulation of proprietary schools is frequently tangential to the central mission of the regulating body and therefore is low on the list of policy priorities for that agency. A partial solution, it notes, could be achieved by increased staffing for regulation of private career schools (New Jersey Interagency Task Force 1990).

Accreditation

Many view accreditation as the "gatekeeper" in the process of institutional eligibility for federal student assistance funds. Though it is actually only one-third of the triad, accreditation's historical function of establishing quality standards has made it the most central aspect of contemporary efforts to reform federal financing of proprietary school training. Therefore, it is useful to briefly review what accreditation is and who performs it in the private career school sector.

Accrediting agencies are private, voluntary associations of member institutions. Without regulatory or enforcement power, their only influence is withdrawal of recognition. Accrediting agencies were originally established to conduct peer reviews of educational quality and to ensure competency for certain types of professional schools. Two types of accreditation are possible: institutional and specialized. The former is concerned with institutionwide objectives, processes, and outcomes, while the latter is concerned more with criteria that relate primarily to requirements for competent professional practice (Jung et al. 1976).

In the case of accreditation for private career schools, determining general institutional quality is the main purpose. Like the case with all accreditation, the process is designed to help schools improve their ability to meet their educational objectives. Accrediting commissions examine quality of the teaching staff, adequacy of the facilities, overall institutional management, student services, the financial health of the school, graduation rates, and placement of graduates. (The last two measures are generally not included in more traditional regional accreditation.) Each accrediting commission has its own set of standards and concerns, however.

Recognition of the accrediting agencies themselves comes from two sources: the U.S. Department of Education and the Council on Postsecondary Accreditation (COPA). Members of accrediting organizations sanctioned by the Department are eligible to participate in federal student aid programs. COPA, on the other hand, is a private organization of accrediting commissions. It recognizes those that it considers legitimate accrediting organizations in their respective fields, coordinates accreditation, and provides national leadership on matters involving accreditation (Young 1987).

Several organizations accredit proprietary schools. Most are involved in institutional accreditation, though some focus strictly on specialized accrediting. These organizations, and their approval status with the Department of Education and COPA, are shown in table 14. Other accrediting organizations, including some of the regional commissions that accredit colleges and universities, also accredit private career schools.

The formal process of accreditation varies by agency. Generally, schools cannot apply for accreditation until they have operated successfully for at least two years. Schools usually file an application with the commission, pay a fee, and then conduct a self-study report based on commission guidelines. Following the self-study (which can take several months), a team, composed by the commission, visits the institution. The commission uses the team's report and a rejoinder from the school to arrive at its decision. Schools typically are either granted accreditation, given provisional accreditation or deferred status, or are denied accreditation.

The pivotal policy question in discussions about accreditation is whether the standards established by the organizations are sufficient. One issue of accreditation that has yet to be resolved, however, is what its primary function should be. The U.S. Department of Education, which relies on approved accrediting organizations as an important factor in the institutional eligibility process for student aid, considers their cen-

TABLE 14

APPROVAL STATUS FOR ACCREDITING ORGANIZATIONS

	U.S. Dept. of Education	COPA
Accrediting Commission of AICS	Yes	Yes
Accrediting Commission of NATTS	Yes	Yes
Accrediting Bureau of Health Education Schools	Yes	Yes
Accrediting Council for Continuing Education and Training	Yes	No
Committee on Allied Health Education and Accreditation	Yes	Yes
National Accreditation Commission on Cosmetology Arts and Sciences	Yes	No
National Home Study Council	Yes	Yes
Board of Review for Baccalaureate and Higher Degree, Associate Degree, Diploma, and Practical Nursing Programs	Yes	Yes

Source: "Accreditation of Proprietary Schools" 1989.

tral mission to be one of certifying that an institution has met established standards of quality. Conversely, accrediting organizations and the academic community in general tend to view accrediting as a process of institutional and program self-improvement—in effect, certifying that the institution is meeting its own stated purposes. Thus, when the Department of Education released new regulations governing approval of accrediting agencies in 1987, the higher education community generally reacted negatively (Uehling 1987).

Though "performance" measures for accrediting organizations are hard to come by, a movement has occurred within the accrediting community toward tightening standards for both accreditation and reaccreditation. NATTS, for example, reports that 11 percent of the schools seeking accreditation through it in 1988 were denied. It also reports that 5 percent of the schools seeking reaccreditation—which occurs about every five years—were also denied, noting that these denials represent a stricter set of standards compared to previous years (Carson 1989).

Some discussion within the accrediting community has also revolved around differential standards across accrediting organizations. Some are concerned that schools that might have difficulty in achieving accredited status simply "shop" for an agency they perceive to have weaker standards, a concern raised in a recent report (California Postsecondary Education Commission 1989b). The chair of the AICS Board of Commissioners also referred to this problem when he wrote that the questionable practices of some agencies have been the subject of concern for his organization, especially those that "have been perceived by some . . . members as actively soliciting institutions for accreditation" (South 1987, p. 10). Recent legislation requires a one-year waiting period before a school that has been denied accreditation by one agency can seek accreditation by another.

Another concern that has been raised is whether accrediting bodies that are related to larger trade associations (like AICS and NATTS) have difficulty implementing stricter standards. Operationally and legally, they are separate organizations, but they do have overlapping membership. The apparent willingness of some schools that have been denied accreditation to seek judicial redress has been noted as one possible hindrance to more rapid and equitable improvements in standards (Mingle 1989). The loss of accreditation means loss of access to student aid, which is tantamount to going out of business. This issue clearly deserves more careful study.

Most formal site visits are scheduled every five years. Intermediary returns can be triggered by complaints from students, the state, or a federal agency, to counter the possibility that schools are on their best behavior only for the accreditation team's visit. NATTS and others have suggested that random unannounced visits be implemented to provide further assurance of ongoing quality.

If the function of accreditation is to certify institutional quality, then it would be helpful to know how effective accrediting organizations are in ferreting out schools with poor or unacceptable practices. Traditionally, accrediting agencies have not included management of student aid. Until the federal government, the states, and the accrediting organizations agree about the proper role for accreditation, however, little will be gained by looking to accreditation as the sole solution to institutional misuse of federal student aid programs.

Federal oversight and monitoring
The third leg of the triad is the federal government. The Department of Education has regulations applying to all

schools participating in Title IV programs that cover institutional eligibility to participate in Title IV programs and recognition of accrediting bodies.

To be eligible for federal student aid, a school must be licensed by the state and accredited by a recognized body. In addition, the school must have been in operation for two years and have courses of at least 300 hours in length. The Department reviews the school's financial strength and administrative capabilities as a condition of approval. If a school has a high default rate, it must have a default reduction plan on file with the Department. All vocational schools are required to file student disclosure information with the Department. This licensing process is repeated for schools every four years. The Department has terminated 35 proprietary schools from participation over the last two years (Schenet 1990).

In addition to the eligibility process, the Department of Education carries out oversight and monitoring. Program reviews, lasting one week, are supposed to be carried out every three years in all schools participating in Title IV programs. These reviews are concerned with the management of federal student aid programs. In 1989, the Department completed about 600 reviews.

Every school is also required to submit to a federal program audit by an independent auditor. If the Department suspects criminal violations, the Inspector General may investigate it (the FBI can investigate cases of mail fraud across state lines). The law also charges guarantee agencies with monitoring schools that participate in the GSL program.

Other agencies have regulations influencing schools. For example, the Federal Aviation Administration certifies schools for airline maintenance technicians, the Veterans Administration regulates schools attended by veterans, and the FTC has the right to investigate complaints against individual schools.

SUMMARY AND CONCLUSIONS

In many ways and for several reasons, proprietary schools are the invisible partners in postsecondary education. One reason for their invisibility is that the participation of private career schools in federal student aid programs began fairly recently with the passage of the 1972 Amendments to the Higher Education Act, which gave these schools equal status with traditional colleges and universities in the receipt of federal funds. Many analysts did not notice the sharp increase in financial aid to students in proprietary schools until the 1980s.

Another reason for reduced visibility is that the narrower vocational training mission of private career schools often makes what they do appear quite different from the liberal arts mission of colleges and universities. Still another is that the profit-making motive of the schools and the fact that many school owners are first and foremost business executives leave proprietary schools and traditional higher education with few shared traditions. For these and other reasons, higher education has on the whole paid little attention to the private career school sector.

Higher education's attention was aroused during the mid-1980s, when widespread public discussion about increases in the dollar amount of defaulted federally insured student loans began to surface. The finger was quickly pointed at proprietary schools, which in many cases were shown to have default rates twice as high as those at other postsecondary institutions, in turn leading to discussions about the private career school sector's "encroachment" on federal student aid programs. In academic year 1987–88, they received more than one-quarter of all Pell grants, more than one-third of all Stafford student loans, and more than one-half of all supplemental loans for students.

The need for accurate and unbiased information about proprietary schools soon became apparent to policy makers and analysts. Unfortunately, because of their traditional "outsider" status, private career schools have rarely been included in the surveys, censuses, and reports about postsecondary education. Much of what is known about proprietary schools is therefore fragmentary and suggestive rather than inclusive and definitive.

Clearly, more accurate and timely information about private career schools and their operation, students, and program offerings must be gathered. Even simple information about the number of schools and students would help. Still, some

... higher education has on the whole paid little attention to the private career school sector.

facts about these schools have been compiled over the years, and the literature provides some clues about the overall nature and scope of the sector.

Proprietary schools have a history dating back more than two centuries. Their development has somewhat paralleled the industrial and technological revolutions of the past century. But the private career schools of old can still be seen in their modern successors, especially in the methods of student recruitment and market analysis.

After World War II, the proprietary school sector of postsecondary education began to blossom. The GI Bill, generally credited with helping millions of students get college degrees, also helped to finance the training of many students in private career schools. The eligibility of proprietary schools as recipients of funds from the GI Bill was not without controversy, however, as government regulators and others singled out some schools for abusive business and educational practices.

With the passage of the Higher Education Act of 1965 and its goal of equality of educational opportunity for those desiring to pursue education after high school came a concurrent interest in supporting students enrolled in vocational programs, including those at private career schools. In the late 1960s, Congress concluded that the separate student aid programs for academic and vocational postsecondary education were quite similar in nature and decided in 1972 to combine both into a single program. At the same time, the Pell Grant program was created, guaranteeing a floor of financial support for low-income students. The unresolved issues regarding the combination of both sectors of postsecondary education into one for federal student aid have contributed to the current intensity of interest in proprietary schools.

In thinking about what private career schools are and what they do, one finds that they are frequently compared with traditional higher education institutions. Indeed, some similarities are apparent; for example, some proprietary schools grant degrees. In most cases, however, private career schools stand alone, with their own traditions and methods. Their profit-making status, decision-making processes, and curricula all reflect their special outlook and distinguish them from their collegiate counterparts.

It is difficult to generalize about how the proprietary sector operates, in part because it is so diverse. Curricula at private career schools can vary from sophisticated, high-technology education to entry-level training. Programs vary in length from a few weeks to several years. Some common threads exist, however. Most proprietary school programs are divided into discrete sequential units. Programs also typically have a more specific vocational focus compared to traditional colleges.

The size and location of schools also cover a wide spectrum. Schools can range from four to 6,000 students on any one campus, with an average enrollment of about 378. Total enrollment in accredited private career schools in 1987 was 1,390,164, based on a universe of 3,949 accredited institutions. New York and California combined make up one-quarter of this total enrollment. Many proprietary schools are found in urban areas.

Faculty at private career schools are generally hired from industry. They usually have less academic training than teachers in the collegiate sector, and their rate of turnover is higher, partly because of the lack of a tenure system. Administrative staff at proprietary schools play a different function from those in other postsecondary institutions. More staff are devoted to admissions and job placement, fewer to infrastructure or auxiliary services, compared to colleges and universities.

Many studies have examined the demographics and socioeconomic status of private career school students. Proprietary school students tend to have less income than those in colleges and universities, are predominantly female, and are more likely to be members of a minority group. They are also somewhat older and more frequently are financially independent of their parents than other postsecondary students.

According to surveys done mostly in the 1970s and early 1980s, a high percentage of private career school students is enrolled in business and secretarial schools. These students tend to be concentrated in computer-oriented courses and programs teaching office skills. Those in trade and technical schools are found in automotive, electrical, and other traditional trade programs, as well as in the allied health fields.

One of the most important questions asked in the ongoing policy discussions about proprietary schools is how well they perform. The outcomes of private career school education are important, especially to those who are concerned about the use of federal student aid funds to train students for specific jobs. Unfortunately, limited research has been done on the outcomes of postsecondary education in general and pro-

prietary schools in particular. Therefore, what is known is fragmentary and inexact, and care should be taken in interpreting the findings of most studies. Better information on graduation rates and postgraduate activities need to be developed for all sectors before conclusions are reached.

Another problem with examining measures of outcomes for private career school students is the difficulty of comparisons with other sectors. Comparing outcomes of proprietary education to other sectors of postsecondary education may be inappropriate, because students in other sectors may be enrolled in longer programs or intend to transfer to another school. Students' characteristics might be related more to outcomes than to institutional factors. And a school enrolling inner-city students might have lower completion rates than a similar program in the suburbs.

Information compiled by the National Assessment of Vocational Education, using data obtained from longitudinal surveys, suggests that rates of completion for proprietary school students have remained unchanged since the early 1970s, have increased for public technical institutes, but have decreased for community colleges. A study of the high school class of 1980 shows that private career school students and those enrolled in four-year programs have similar completion rates, though the data may not be comparable.

In terms of economic and employment outcomes, several studies suggest that some proprietary school students are not satisfied with their training. NAVE found that private career school graduates appear to have a higher incidence of unemployment than those in other postsecondary vocational programs and earn at least the same hourly wages as their counterparts in other vocational sectors.

Aside from outcomes, many important policy issues have been explored in the literature. One is the use of student aid by proprietary school students. The 1987 NPSAS documented those students' reliance on student aid. Approximately 81 percent of private career school students receive some form of student aid, and 76 percent receive federal assistance—in both instances, virtually twice the level of all postsecondary students. Students in colleges receive much more assistance from state and private sources compared to proprietary students, however.

The percentage of dollars in federal student aid programs going to proprietary school students increased from almost nothing in 1972 to $4 billion in 1990. The share of federal dollars per student, according to NPSAS figures for 1987, was $5,633 for private college students, $4,025 for proprietary school students, and $2,887 for public college students. Private career school students get little aid from nonfederal sources.

The federal policy debate has centered on the fact that proprietary school students have much higher rates of default than other students. The voluminous literature that has arisen as a result of this interest in the topic suggests that default is a complex matter with few easy answers. The literature indicates that rates of default in general have not varied substantially since the mid-1970s but that significant increases in dollars borrowed have pushed annual dollars entering default to levels unacceptable in the policy world—at least $1 billion a year since 1985 and approaching $2 billion in 1990.

Studies concerned with the individual characteristics of borrowers who default show that an inverse relationship exists between default and indebtedness, that borrowers in their first few years of repayment are more likely to default, and that dropping out and low family income are both correlated with defaulting. Those studies that attempt to isolate the effect of institutional type on defaulting suggest that these characteristics help to explain why private career school borrowers default more frequently than students in other sectors.

If the characteristics of proprietary school students cannot entirely explain why they default at higher rates than other students, then perhaps other reasons related to institutional management might account for such differences. Regrettably, those studies that examine violation of students' consumer rights usually cannot ascertain the extent of such abuses more than simply their correlation with default. The studies usually concentrate on classifying abuse and suggesting remedies rather than on exploring its pervasiveness.

One study explored a field of consumer rights, the use of "ability-to-benefit" provisions in federal law to admit students without a high school diploma or equivalent to a postsecondary program (Sango-Jordan 1988). Using the 1987 NPSAS data set, the researcher found that about 9 percent of all private career school students were admitted to programs based on ability-to-benefit standards. More research in this and other areas of potential consumer abuse is necessary.

Consumer rights are generally believed to be protected through state licensing and accreditation of proprietary schools. Accreditation and licensing, together with federal program certification, are often referred to as the triad system of determining eligibility for federal student aid programs, and state licensing, private accreditation, and federal regulation should therefore play an important role in protecting students from unscrupulous school operators and misuse of student aid.

Each state has some form of structure to oversee planning and policy development for private career schools; however, the structural types vary considerably by state. Typically, states divide consideration of proprietary school oversight between degree-granting versus non-degree-granting institutions. Degree-granting schools are usually regulated by the same agency that regulates higher education institutions—a department of higher education in many states. Non-degree-granting schools, which make up the majority of the private career school sector, are usually regulated by other state agencies.

States' regulation of proprietary schools is complicated by the fact that multiple state agencies have varying responsibilities for different kinds of private career schools and programs. In about two-thirds of the states, licensing authority for non-degree-granting schools is vested in the state department of education. It is not unusual, however, for states to also vest some licensing authority in a cosmetology board (for cosmetology schools) or in several other state agencies (such as a department of motor vehicles for schools teaching truck driving). This arrangement has served to complicate attempts in several states to tighten licensing standards.

State licensing serves three central functions: It establishes minimum educational standards to which all schools must adhere; it requires schools to meet minimum financial criteria to protect the state's financial interest in the schools (through student aid or vocational training programs); and it protects schools and students from unfair competition. It also shields the student from fraudulent recruiting practices. States have numerous ways of fulfilling these duties, and they vary a great deal in how they exercise their responsibilities in this area.

Most of the discussion about state regulation of proprietary schools is concerned with weaknesses in existing laws and rules. The most common problems include inadequate surety bonding of schools (to reimburse students for lost tuition in the event of the school's sudden closure), legal obstacles that frequently prevent states from enforcing existing laws, and many states' exempting accredited schools from a full licensure review. Poor enforcement of existing laws, partly the result of the relative obscurity of private career school units in large state agencies and low staffing levels, is also a recurring problem for states.

Accreditation—often seen as the "gatekeeper" for federal student aid because of the historical role played by accrediting associations in establishing standards of quality—is conducted by private, voluntary organizations. Accrediting commissions evaluate institutional management, the school's financial health, and its educational quality. Each accrediting agency has its own set of standards and concerns and must be approved by the U.S. Department of Education.

A policy question has been raised about whether standards established by the accrediting agencies are adequate to ensure quality in private career schools. This question points to the larger concern: What is the primary function of accreditation? The U.S. Department of Education assumes that accreditation certifies that an institution has met established standards of quality, but accrediting organizations and the academic community generally tend to view accreditation as a process of institutional and program self-improvement.

With this fundamental disagreement, it is difficult to evaluate how accrediting organizations have "performed" and whether that performance is sufficient, because the needs of the two agencies are different. Still, some important questions have been raised. Concern has been raised, for example, that accrediting organizations' differing standards make federal reliance on accreditation as a condition for eligibility for student aid tenuous. Concern has also been raised as to whether accrediting organizations related to trade associations can effectively improve their standards. Accreditation standards and their enforcement among the different accreditation groups have not been directly compared. Such a study could help clarify this discussion.

The assembled body of knowledge concerning proprietary schools offers much for the reader interested in thinking about the role these schools play in postsecondary education. The diversity of profit-making schools presents problems for the analyst wishing to generalize about the sector. The data, studies, and analyses indicate that no simple conclusions can be reached about the sector. Studies attribute both positive and negative values to private career schools. They play a vari-

. . . it is imperative that all parties with a stake in the debate about proprietary schools initiate better research.

ety of roles in the postsecondary education sector, from providing an educational alternative for marginal students to introducing students to the most sophisticated technology. Their relationship with other players in the system is tenuous, because they compete for money and students.

A certain level of frustration also exists with the literature, however, because of what it does not say or cannot answer. For this reason, it is imperative that all parties with a stake in the debate about proprietary schools initiate better research.

The rest of postsecondary education and the public at large will probably continue to treat private career schools as outsiders for the foreseeable future. But the fact remains that proprietary schools play an important part in the education of students and in the allocation of federal funds to support postsecondary students. This review of the proprietary sector and the programs and policies affecting it only begins to explore the many issues that need to be addressed. It represents just the beginning of a long and probably difficult road toward understanding the role proprietary schools play in postsecondary education and the path they might pursue in the future.

REFERENCES

The Educational Resources Information Center (ERIC) Clearinghouse
on Higher Education abstracts and indexes the current literature on
higher education for inclusion in ERIC's data base and announce-
ment in ERIC's monthly bibliographic journal, *Resources in Education* (RIE). Most of these publications are available through the
ERIC Document Reproduction Service (EDRS). For publications cited
in this bibliography that are available from EDRS, ordering number
and price code are included. Readers who wish to order a publication should write to the ERIC Document Reproduction Service,
3900 Wheeler Avenue, Alexandria, Virginia 22304. (Phone orders
with VISA or MasterCard are taken at 800/227-ERIC or 703/823-0500.)
When ordering, please specify the document (ED) number. Documents are available as noted in microfiche (MF) and paper copy
(PC). If you have the price code ready when you call EDRS, an exact
price can be quoted. The last page of the latest issue of *Resources
in Education* also has the current cost, listed by code.

"Accreditation of Proprietary Schools." October 1989. *Maryland Asso-
ciation for Higher Education Journal* 13: 15–23.
"ACE Chief Seeks Separate Trade-School Aid Programs." 1 February
1989. *Chronicle of Higher Education:* A19.
Apling, Richard N., and Steven R. Aleman. 1990. *Proprietary Schools:
A Description of Institutions and Students.* Washington, D.C.: Con-
gressional Research Service.
Banerjee, Neela, Ying Zhou, and Christina Caruso. 1989. *Unfair at
Any Price: Welfare Recipients at New York Proprietary Schools.*
New York: Interface Development Project, Inc.
Bauman, David. 22 October 1990. "House-Senate Agreement Would
Phase in Loan Cutoff." *Education Daily* 23: 1–2.
Belitsky, A. Harvey. 1969. *Private Vocational Schools and Their Stu-
dents: Limited Objectives, Unlimited Opportunities.* Cambridge,
Mass.: Schenkman Publishing Co.
Bender, Louis W. 1973. "Education Commission of the States: A
Report of the Task Force." In *Model State Legislation.* Denver: Edu-
cation Commission of the States. ED 083 896. 51 pp. MF–01;
PC–03.
———. 1976. "Licensing/Approval Organization Structure for the
Fifty States, Covering Private and Proprietary Degree-Granting and
Non-Degree-Granting Institutions." Paper presented at the Edu-
cation Commission of the States/State Higher Education Executive
Officers Seminar for State Leaders in Postsecondary Education,
July, Keystone, Colorado. ED 202 298. 18 pp. MF–01; PC–01.
Bolino, August C. 1973. *Career Education: Contributions to Eco-
nomic Growth.* New York: Praeger.
California Postsecondary Education Commission. 1985. *Mortgaging
a Generation: Problems and Prospects for California's Guaranteed
Student Loan Program.* Sacramento: California Education Loan

Program. ED 259 661. 111 pp. MF–01; PC–05.

————. 1989a. *Recommendations for Revising the Private Postsecondary Act of 1977.* Sacramento: Author.

————. 1989b. "The State's Reliance on Nongovernmental Accreditation." Report to the legislature in response to assembly concurrent resolution 78. Sacramento: Author.

California Student Aid Commission. 1988. *Student Borrowing in California.* Sacramento: Author.

Career Training Foundation. 1991. *A Description of Private Career School Students Who Do Not Have a High School Diploma.* Washington, D.C.: Author. Forthcoming.

Carson, William C. 29 March 1989. "Majority of Private Trade Schools Are a Success." *New York Times.*

Chaloux, Bruce N. 1985. "State Oversight of the Private and Proprietary Sector." Paper presented at a joint session of the National Association of Trade and Technical Schools and the Association of Independent Colleges and Schools, April 19, Miami, Florida. ED 270 060. 38 pp. MF–01; PC–02.

Choy, Susan P., and Antoinette G. Gifford. 1990. *Profile of Undergraduates in American Postsecondary Institutions.* Washington, D.C.: U.S. Dept. of Education, Office of Educational Research and Improvement. HE 023 900. 180 pp. MF–01; PC–08.

Christian, C.E. 1975. "Analysis of a Pilot Survey of Proprietary Schools." Los Angeles: Higher Education Research Institute.

Clark, Harold F., and Harold S. Sloan. 1966. *Classrooms on Main Street.* New York: Teachers College Press.

College Board. 1990. *Trends in Student Aid: 1980–1989.* New York: Author.

Davis, Jerry S. 1984. "Guaranteed Student Loan Program Default Rates and Volumes by States for Fiscal Years 1981, 1982, and 1983: A Brief Report and Comparison of Patterns and Trends." Harrisburg: Pennsylvania Higher Education Assistance Agency.

————. 1985. "Ten Facts about Defaults in the Guaranteed Student Loan Program." Harrisburg: Pennsylvania Higher Education Assistance Agency.

Downes, John M. 1991. "Ability-to-Benefit Students Attending NATTS Schools." Washington, D.C.: Career Training Foundation. Forthcoming.

Education Commission of the States. 1973. *Model State Legislation: A Report of the Task Force.* Denver: Author.

Ehlenfeldt, Lisa L., and Donna Springfield. 1984. "Study of Guaranteed Student Loan Default Rates." Richmond: Virginia Education Loan Authority.

Evelyn, Kay R. 1971. *Vocational Education: Characteristics of Teachers and Students, 1969.* Washington, D.C.: U.S. Dept. of Health, Education, and Welfare. ED 050 297. 82 pp. MF–01; PC not available EDRS.

Federal Trade Commission. 1976. "Proprietary Vocational and Home Study Schools." Final report to the Federal Trade Commission on the Proposed Trade Study Rule. 16 CFR 438. Washington, D.C.: U.S. Government Printing Office.

Fitzgerald, Brian, and Lisa Harmon. 1988. "Consumer Rights and Accountability in Postsecondary Vocational-Technical Education: An Exploratory Study." Report prepared for the Office of Planning, Budget, and Evaluation, U.S. Dept. of Education. Washington, D.C.: Pelavin Associates, Inc.

Freeman, Richard B. 1974. "Occupational Training in Proprietary Schools and Technical Institutes." *Review of Economics and Statistics* 56: 310–18.

Friedlander, Marci Cox. 1980. *Characteristics of Students Attending Proprietary Schools and Factors Influencing Their Institutional Choice.* Cincinnati: South-Western Publishing Co.

Goodwin, David. 1989. *Postsecondary Vocational Education: Final Report.* Vol. 4. Washington, D.C.: National Assessment of Vocational Education.

Greenberg, Joseph A., and Hossein Torabi. 1985. "Characteristics of Trade and Technical Students and Schools." *Career Training* 2(2): 30–32.

Hall, Herman S. 1930. *Trade Training in School and Plant.* New York: Century.

Hauptman, Arthur M. 1983. "ACE Policy Brief: Student Loan Default Rates in Perspective." Washington, D.C.: American Council on Education.

Hauptman, Arthur M., and Jamie P. Merisotis. 1989. "Issues in Postsecondary Education and Training." In *Investing in People: A Strategy to Address America's Workforce Crisis.* Washington, D.C.: U.S. Dept. of Labor, Commission on Workforce Quality and Labor Market Efficiency.

Herrick, Chessman A. 1904. *Meaning and Practice of Commercial Education.* New York: Macmillan.

Hill, David S. 1920. *An Introduction to Vocational Education.* New York: Macmillan.

Hyde, William D., Jr. 1976. *Metropolitan Vocational Proprietary Schools.* Lexington, Mass.: Lexington Books.

ITT Educational Services. 1982. *America at Work: The Evolving Role of Proprietary Vocational Education.* Indianapolis: Author. ED 223 892. 59 pp. MF–01; PC–03.

Jones, Maurice. 1987. "The Significance of State Licensing." *Career Training* 3(3): 15–17.

Jung, Steven M. 1980. "Proprietary Vocational Education." In *Information Series No. 197.* Washington, D.C.: U.S. Dept. of Health, Education, and Welfare, National Center for Research in Vocational Education. ED 186 760. 49 pp. MF–01; PC–02.

Jung, Steven M., and Jack A. Hamilton, Carolyn B. Helliwell, and others. 1976. *Improving the Consumer Protection Function in Post-secondary Education.* Final Technical Report. Washington, D.C.: U.S. Dept. of Health, Education, and Welfare, Office of Education.

Katz, H.H. 1973. *A State-of-the-Art Study on the Independent Private School Industry in the State of Illinois.* Springfield: Illinois Advisory Council on Vocational Education.

Korb, Roslyn, Nancy Schantz, Peter Stowe, and Linda Zimbler. 1988. *Undergraduate Financing of Postsecondary Education: A Report of the 1987 National Postsecondary Student Aid Study.* Washington, D.C.: U.S. Dept. of Education, National Center for Education Statistics. ED 295 531. 206 pp. MF–01; PC–09.

Laoria, Gail Hentz. 1984. *A Summary of New Jersey Private Vocational Business Schools and Their Impact on the Business Community.* Cincinnati: South-Western Publishing Co.

Lee, John B. 1982. "Study of Guaranteed Student Loan Default Rates." Washington, D.C.: Applied Systems Institute.

———. 1987. "Economically, These Schools Make 'Good Cents'." *Career Training* 4(2): 26–30+.

———. 1988a. *Enrollment in Private Career Schools by State.* Working paper. Denver: Education Commission of the States, Task Force on State Policy and Independent Higher Education.

———. 1988b. "Stafford Loan Defaults and Private Career Schools." Washington, D.C.: Career Training Foundation.

———. 1990a. "Enrollment Sequence of Private Career School Students." Washington, D.C.: Career Training Foundation.

———. 1990b. "Private Career Schools and the Labor Market: A Supply-and-Demand Relationship." Washington, D.C.: Career Training Foundation.

———. 1990c. "Who Defaults on Their Student Loans?" *Career Training* 6(3): 30–33.

Lee, John B., and William Munn. 1988. "An Overview of the Cosmetology Industry." Washington, D.C.: National Association of Accredited Cosmetology Schools.

McClure, Barbara. 1986. "Veterans Education Assistance Programs." Report No. 86-32 EPW. Washington, D.C.: Congressional Research Service.

MacKenzie, Ossian, et al. 1968. *Correspondence Instruction in the United States.* New York: McGraw-Hill.

Merisotis, Jamie P. 1988. "Default Trends in Major Postsecondary Education Sectors." *Journal of Student Financial Aid* 18(1): 18–28.

———. 1989. "GSL Defaults: A Review of the Literature and Comparison with Other Federally Guaranteed Loan Programs." In *Private Career Schools and the Stafford Student Loan Program.* Washington, D.C.: Career Training Foundation.

Miller, Jay Wilson. 1939. *A Critical Analysis of the Organization, Administration, and Function of the Private Business Schools of the United States.* Cincinnati: South-Western Publishing Co.

Mingle, James R. 1989. "Public Policy and Private Career Schools." Denver: State Higher Education Executive Officers.

National Association of Student Financial Aid Administrators. November 1987. "Guaranteed Student Loan Default Information." *NASFAA Federal Monitor* 166.

New Jersey Interagency Task Force on Proprietary Vocational Schools. 1990. "State Agency Regulation, Oversight, and Funding of Programs at Proprietary Vocational Schools." Trenton: Author.

New York State Education Department. 1989. "Toward a Comprehensive Policy for Approaching Proprietary Vocational School Issues." Albany: Author.

New York State Higher Education Services Corporation. 1984. "Student Loan Payers and Defaulters." Albany: Author.

Noffsinger, J.S. 1926. *Correspondence Schools, Lyceums, and Chautauquas.* New York: Macmillan.

Petrello, George J. 1988. *In Service to America: AICS at 75.* New York: McGraw-Hill.

Reeher, Kenneth R., and Jerry S. Davis. 1989. *20th Annual Survey Report: 1988–89 Academic Year.* Harrisburg, Pa.: National Association of State Scholarship and Grant Programs. ED 305 854. 176 pp. MF–01; PC–08.

Sango-Jordan, Marilyn. 1988. *A Description of Ability-to-Benefit Students from the National Postsecondary Student Aid Study.* Washington, D.C.: Career Training Foundation.

––––––. May 1989. "Private Career School Training: Economic Outcomes." *Career Training* 5: 30–35.

Schaeffer, Donald E. 1979. "Financial Aid at Proprietary Schools: How Important Is It?" *Journal of Student Financial Aid* 9(2): 16–28.

Schenet, Margot A. 1990. *Proprietary Schools: The Regulatory Structure.* Report No. 90-424 EPW. Washington, D.C.: Congressional Research Service.

Scholl, Jayne. 2 January 1989. "Schools for Scandal: Vocational Education Operators Get Poor Marks." *Barron's:* 16+.

South, John T. 1987. "Dual Accreditation." *Career Training* 3(3): 10.

Starr, Paul. 1973. *The Discarded Army: Veterans after Vietnam.* New York: Charterhouse.

Stewart, David W., and Henry A. Spille. 1988. *Diploma Mills: Degrees of Fraud.* New York: American Council on Education/Macmillan.

Tennessee Higher Education Commission. 1989. "Proposed Revision to the Tennessee Postsecondary Education Authorization Act of 1974." Nashville: Author.

Tonne, Herbert A. 1939. *Business Education: Basic Principles and Trends.* New York: Gregg Publishing Co.

––––––. 1954. *Principles of Business Education.* 2d ed. New York: McGraw-Hill.

Uehling, Barbara S. 30 November 1987. "Bennett's Accreditation Proposal: Simplistic and Uninformed." *Higher Education and*

National Affairs (36)23.

U.S. Congress, House of Representatives. 1965. *National Vocational Student Loan Insurance Act of 1965.* House Report No. 308. 89th Congress, First Session. Washington, D.C.: U.S. Government Printing Office.

————, Subcommittee on Education and Health of the Joint Economic Committee. 1988. "A Cost Benefit Analysis of Government Investment in Postsecondary Education under World War II GI Bill." Washington, D.C.: Author.

U.S. Department of Education, National Center for Education Statistics. 1982. *Postsecondary Schools with Occupational Programs, 1982.* Washington, D.C.: Author. ED 236 407. 353 pp. MF–01; PC–15.

————. 1987. *1987 National Postsecondary Student Aid Study.* Washington, D.C.: Author.

————. 1988. *Digest of Education Statistics, 1988.* Washington, D.C.: Author. ED 295 344. 469 pp. MF–01; PC–19.

————. 1991. *Consumer Rights Information in Postsecondary Education: An Overview of State Data Collection Activities.* Washington, D.C.: Author. Forthcoming.

U.S. General Accounting Office. 1989. *Supplemental Loans for Students: Who Borrows and Who Defaults.* GAO/HRD-90-33FS. Washington, D.C.: Author. ED 314 000. 25 pp. MF–01; PC–01.

Wilms, Wellford W. 1976. *Public and Proprietary Vocational Training: A Study of Effectiveness.* Lexington, Mass.: Lexington Books.

————. 1982. *Proprietary Vocational Schools: A Significant Sector of American Postsecondary Education.* Washington, D.C.: National Commission on Student Financial Assistance. ED 228 942. 32 pp. MF–01; PC–02.

Wilms, Wellford W., Richard W. Moore, and Roger E. Bolus. 1986. "Explaining Defaults: A Study of Students, Schools, and Lenders." Sacramento: California Student Aid Commission.

————. 1987. "Whose Fault Is Default?" *Educational Evaluation and Policy Analysis* 9(1): 41–54.

Wolfe, Mark, David Osman, and Vic Miller. 1987. *Report on Federal Guaranteed Student Loan Default Rates by Institutions of Postsecondary Education.* Washington, D.C.: Federal Funds Information for States.

Wolman, J.M., V.N. Campbell, S.M. Jung, and J.M. Richards. 1972. *A Comparative Study of Proprietary and Nonproprietary Vocational Training Programs.* 2 vols. Palo Alto, Cal.: American Institutes for Research. Vol. 1: ED 067 523. 130 pp. MF–01; PC–06. Vol. 2: ED 067 524. 154 pp. MF–01; PC–07.

Yin, Robert K. 1988. "Comments on Methodology Used in Paper on 'Consumer Rights and Accountability' by Pelavin Associates." Washington, D.C.: Career Training Foundation.

Young, Kenneth E. 1987. "Accrediting Organizations: You Can't Tell the Players without a Program." *Career Training* 3(3): 8–10.

INDEX

A

Accredited proprietary schools, 22, 23
Accreditation
    proprietary schools, 67-70
Association of Independent Colleges and Schools, 8

B

Bacon, R. C., 5
Bacon's Mercantile Colleges, 5
Bartlett, R. M., 5
Belitsky's Taxonomy of Schools, 13, 19
Bennett, James, 5
Boards of trustees
    nonprofit colleges, 16
Bryant, H. B., 5
Bryant-Stratton Schools, 5, 6
Bureau of the Budget, 10

C

California
    student loan defaults, 55
California Student Aid Commission, 55
Centennial Exposition, 7
Classification of instructional programs, 19
College work study, 46
Community colleges, 12
Completion rates
    proprietary schools, 35, 38
Consumer rights and abuses, 58, 60-62
Correspondence instruction, 4
Council on Postsecondary Education, 68
Curricula
    private schools, 18-20

D

Decision making
    proprietary schools, 15
Defaults
    student loan programs, 45, 49-58
Degree granting
    proprietary schools, 14, 15
Duff, Peter, 5

E

Earnings
    proprietary school graduates, 41
Eastman, H. G., 6

Economic outcomes
proprietary schools, 39
Education quality
private career schools, 35
Employment outcomes
proprietary schools, 39
Enrollment
proprietary schools, 23, 32, 35

F

Federal Trade Commission, 59
Forbes Commercial School, 5

G

Gardner Lyceum, 4
General Accounting Office, 10
GI Bill, 49
Governmental assistance, 45
Gregg, John, 7
Guaranteed Student Loan Program, 11

H

Hall, Herman S., 2
High School and Beyond Survey of the Class of 1980, 36
Higher Education Act, 11
amendments, 13
Higher Education Research Institute, 27
History of proprietary school education, 4

I

Illinois
student loan defaults, 55
Income
postsecondary students, 42

J

Job Training Partnership Act, 49
Jones, Jonathan, 5

L

Land Grant Act, 7
Licensing
proprietary schools, 63
states, 63-67
Lyceum Movement, 4

M

Massachusetts

student loan defaults, 55

N

National Accrediting Commission of Cosmetology Arts and Sciences, 9

National Assessment of Vocational Education, 37

National Association of Accredited Commercial Schools, 8

National Association of Trade and Technical Schools, 9

National Center for Education Statistics, 36

National Council of Business Schools, 9

National Defense Student Loan program, 11

National Home Study Council, 24

National Longitudinal Survey of the Class of 1972, 36

National Postsecondary Student Aid Study, 29

National Vocational Student Loan Insurance Act, 11

New Jersey
    student loan defaults, 55

New York City
    proprietary schools, 40

O

Office of Education, 8

P

Parent loans for undergraduate students, 46

Pell Grant, 13, 46, 47

Pennsylvania
    student loan defaults, 55

Perkins Loan, 46

Phillips, Caleb, 4

Policy
    postsecondary education, 45

Private career schools
    versus traditional higher education, 14

Private resident schools, 4

Programs
    trade and technical schools, 20

Proprietary school associations, 8

Proprietary schools
    critics, 2
    Federal oversight and monitoring, 70, 71
    licensing and accreditation, 62
    post World War II, 10
    size and location, 4
    staffing and pay, 24, 25
    supporters, 2

ASHE-ERIC HIGHER EDUCATION REPORTS

Since 1983, the Association for the Study of Higher Education (ASHE) and the Educational Resources Information Center (ERIC) Clearinghouse on Higher Education, a sponsored project of the School of Education and Human Development at The George Washington University, have cosponsored the *ASHE-ERIC Higher Education Report* series. The 1990 series is the nineteenth overall and the second to be published by the School of Education and Human Development at the George Washington University.

Each monograph is the definitive analysis of a tough higher education problem, based on thorough research of pertinent literature and insitutional experiences. Topics are identified by a national survey. Noted practitioners and scholars are then commissioned to write the reports, with experts providing critical reviews of each manuscript before publication.

Eight monographs (10 before 1985) in the ASHE-ERIC Higher Education Report series are published each year and are available on individual and subscription basis. Subscription to eight issues is $80.00 annually; $60 to members of AAHE, AIR, or AERA; and $50 to ASHE members. All foreign subscribers must include an additional $10 per series year for postage.

To order single copies of existing reports, use the order form on the last page of this book. Regular prices, and special rates available to members of AAHE, AIR, AERA and ASHE, are as follows:

Series	Regular	Members
1990	$17.00	$12.75
1988-89	15.00	11.25
1985-87	10.00	7.50
1983-84	7.50	6.00
before 1983	6.50	5.00

Price includes book rate postage within the U.S. For foreign orders, please add $1.00 per book. Fast United Parcel Service available within the contiguous U.S. at $2.50 for each order under $50.00, and calculated at 5% of invoice total for orders $50.00 or above.

All orders under $45.00 must be prepaid. Make check payable to ASHE-ERIC. For Visa or MasterCard, include card number, expiration date and signature. A bulk discount of 10% is available on orders of 15 or more books (not applicable on subscriptions).

Address order to
ASHE-ERIC Higher Education Reports
The George Washington University
1 Dupont Circle, Suite 630
Washington, DC 20036
Or phone (202) 296-2597

Write or call for a complete catalog of ASHE-ERIC Higher Education Reports.

1990 ASHE-ERIC Higher Education Reports

1. The Campus Green: Fund Raising in Higher Education
   Barbara E. Brittingham and Thomas R. Pezzullo

2. The Emeritus Professor: Old Rank - New Meaning
   James E. Mauch, Jack W. Birch, and Jack Matthews

3. "High Risk" Students in Higher Education: Future Trends
   Dionne J. Jones and Betty Collier Watson

4. Budgeting for Higher Education at the State Level: Enigma, Paradox, and Ritual
   Daniel T. Layzell and Jan W. Lyddon

1989 ASHE-ERIC Higher Education Reports

1. Making Sense of Administrative Leadership: The 'L' Word in Higher Education
   Estela M. Bensimon, Anna Neumann, and Robert Birnbaum

2. Affirmative Rhetoric, Negative Action: African-American and Hispanic Faculty at Predominantly White Universities
   Valora Washington and William Harvey

3. Postsecondary Developmental Programs: A Traditional Agenda with New Imperatives
   Louise M. Tomlinson

4. The Old College Try: Balancing Athletics and Academics in Higher Education
   John R. Thelin and Lawrence L. Wiseman

5. The Challenge of Diversity: Involvement or Alienation in the Academy?
   Daryl G. Smith

6. Student Goals for College and Courses: A Missing Link in Assessing and Improving Academic Achievement
   Joan S. Stark, Kathleen M. Shaw, and Malcolm A. Lowther

7. The Student as Commuter: Developing a Comprehensive Institutional Response
   Barbara Jacoby

8. Renewing Civic Capacity: Preparing College Students for Service and Citizenship
   Suzanne W. Morse

1988 ASHE-ERIC Higher Education Reports

1. The Invisible Tapestry: Culture in American Colleges and Universities
   George D. Kuh and Elizabeth J. Whitt

2. Critical Thinking: Theory, Research, Practice, and Possibilities
   Joanne Gainen Kurfiss

3. Developing Academic Programs: The Climate for Innovation
   Daniel T. Seymour

4. Peer Teaching: To Teach is To Learn Twice
   Neal A. Whitman

5. Higher Education and State Governments: Renewed Partnership, Cooperation, or Competition?
   Edward R. Hines

6. Entrepreneurship and Higher Education: Lessons for Colleges, Universities, and Industry
   James S. Fairweather

7. Planning for Microcomputers in Higher Education: Strategies for the Next Generation
   Reynolds Ferrante, John Hayman, Mary Susan Carlson, and Harry Phillips

8. The Challenge for Research in Higher Education: Harmonizing Excellence and Utility
   Alan W. Lindsay and Ruth T. Neumann

1987 ASHE-ERIC Higher Education Reports

1. Incentive Early Retirement Programs for Faculty: Innovative Responses to a Changing Environment
   Jay L. Chronister and Thomas R. Kepple, Jr.

2. Working Effectively with Trustees: Building Cooperative Campus Leadership
   Barbara E. Taylor

3. Formal Recognition of Employer-Sponsored Instruction: Conflict and Collegiality in Postsecondary Education
   Nancy S. Nash and Elizabeth M. Hawthorne

4. Learning Styles: Implications for Improving Educational Practices
   Charles S. Claxton and Patricia H. Murrell

5. Higher Education Leadership: Enhancing Skills through Professional Development Programs
   Sharon A. McDade

6. Higher Education and the Public Trust: Improving Stature in Colleges and Universities
   Richard L. Alfred and Julie Weissman

7. College Student Outcomes Assessment: A Talent Development Perspective
   Maryann Jacobi, Alexander Astin, and Frank Ayala, Jr.

8. Opportunity from Strength: Strategic Planning Clarified with Case Examples
   Robert G. Cope

1986 ASHE-ERIC Higher Education Reports

1. Post-tenure Faculty Evaluation: Threat or Opportunity?
   Christine M. Licata

2. Blue Ribbon Commissions and Higher Education: Changing Academe from the Outside
   Janet R. Johnson and Laurence R. Marcus

3. Responsive Professional Education: Balancing Outcomes and Opportunities
   Joan S. Stark, Malcolm A. Lowther, and Bonnie M.K. Hagerty

4. Increasing Students' Learning: A Faculty Guide to Reducing Stress among Students
   Neal A. Whitman, David C. Spendlove, and Claire H. Clark

5. Student Financial Aid and Women: Equity Dilemma?
   Mary Moran

6. The Master's Degree: Tradition, Diversity, Innovation
   Judith S. Glazer

7. The College, the Constitution, and the Consumer Student: Implications for Policy and Practice
   Robert M. Hendrickson and Annette Gibbs

8. Selecting College and University Personnel: The Quest and the Question
   Richard A. Kaplowitz

1985 ASHE-ERIC Higher Education Reports

1. Flexibility in Academic Staffing: Effective Policies and Practices
   Kenneth P. Mortimer, Marque Bagshaw, and Andrew T. Masland

2. Associations in Action: The Washington, D.C. Higher Education Community
   Harland G. Bloland

3. And on the Seventh Day: Faculty Consulting and Supplemental Income
   Carol M. Boyer and Darrell R. Lewis

4. Faculty Research Performance: Lessons from the Sciences and Social Sciences
   John W. Creswell

5. Academic Program Review: Institutional Approaches, Expectations, and Controversies
   Clifton F. Conrad and Richard F. Wilson

6. Students in Urban Settings: Achieving the Baccalaureate Degree
   Richard C. Richardson, Jr. and Louis W. Bender

7. Serving More Than Students: A Critical Need for College Student Personnel Services
   Peter H. Garland

8. Faculty Participation in Decision Making: Necessity or Luxury?
   Carol E. Floyd

1984 ASHE-ERIC Higher Education Reports

1. Adult Learning: State Policies and Institutional Practices
   K. Patricia Cross and Anne-Marie McCartan

2. Student Stress: Effects and Solutions
   Neal A. Whitman, David C. Spendlove, and Claire H. Clark

3. Part-time Faulty: Higher Education at a Crossroads
   Judith M. Gappa

4. Sex Discrimination Law in Higher Education: The Lessons of the Past Decade. ED 252 169.*
   J. Ralph Lindgren, Patti T. Ota, Perry A. Zirkel, and Nan Van Gieson

5. Faculty Freedoms and Institutional Accountability: Interactions and Conflicts
   Steven G. Olswang and Barbara A. Lee

6. The High Technology Connection: Academic/Industrial Cooperation for Economic Growth
   Lynn G. Johnson

7. Employee Educational Programs: Implications for Industry and Higher Education. ED 258 501.*
   Suzanne W. Morse

8. Academic Libraries: The Changing Knowledge Centers of Colleges and Universities
   Barbara B. Moran

9. Futures Research and the Strategic Planning Process: Implications for Higher Education
   James L. Morrison, William L. Renfro, and Wayne I. Boucher

10. Faculty Workload: Research, Theory, and Interpretation
    Harold E. Yuker

1983 ASHE-ERIC Higher Education Reports

1. The Path to Excellence: Quality Assurance in Higher Education
   Laurence R. Marcus, Anita O. Leone, and Edward D. Goldberg

2. Faculty Recruitment, Retention, and Fair Employment: Obligations and Opportunities
   John S. Waggaman

*Out-of-print. Available through EDRS. Call 1-800-227-ERIC.

ORDER FORM

Quantity   **Amount**

_____ Please send a complete set of the 1989 *ASHE-ERIC Higher Education Reports* at $80.00, 33% off the cover price.   _____

_____ Please begin my subscription to the 1990 *ASHE-ERIC Higher Education Reports* at $80.00, 41% off the cover price, starting with Report 1, 1990   _____

_____ Outside the U.S., add $10 per series for postage   _____

Individual reports are avilable at the following prices:

1990 and forward, $17.00	1983 and 1984, $7.50
1988 and 1989, $15.00	1982 and back, $6.50
1985 to 1987, $10.00	

Book rate postage within the U.S. is included. Outside U.S., please add $1 per book for postage. Fast U.P.S. shipping is available within the contiguous U.S. at $2.50 for each order under $50.00, and calculated at 5% of invoice total for orders $50.00 or above. All orders under $45 must be prepaid.

PLEASE SEND ME THE FOLLOWING REPORTS:

Quantity	Report No.	Year	Title	Amount
			Subtotal:	
			Foreign or UPS:	
			Total Due:	

Please check one of the following:
☐ Check enclosed, payable to GWU-ERIC.
☐ Purchase order attached ($45.00 minimum).
☐ Charge my credit card indicated below:
    ☐ Visa   ☐ MasterCard

Expiration Date _____

Name _____

Title _____

Institution _____

Address _____

City _____ State _____ Zip _____

Phone _____

Signature _____ Date _____

SEND ALL ORDERS TO:
ASHE-ERIC Higher Education Reports
The George Washington University
One Dupont Circle, Suite 630
Washington, DC 20036-1183
Phone: (202) 296-2597